UNIVERSITY OF NORTH CAROLINA AT CHAPEL HILL
DEPARTMENT OF ROMANCE LANGUAGES

NORTH CAROLINA STUDIES
IN THE ROMANCE LANGUAGES AND LITERATURES

Founder: URBAN TIGNER HOLMES
Editor: MARÍA A. SALGADO

Distributed by:

UNIVERSITY OF NORTH CAROLINA PRESS
CHAPEL HILL
North Carolina 27515-2288
U.S.A.

NORTH CAROLINA STUDIES IN THE
ROMANCE LANGUAGES AND LITERATURES
Number 238

IMPERMANENT STRUCTURES

IMPERMANENT STRUCTURES
Semiotic Readings of Nelson Rodrigues'
Vestido de noiva, Álbum de família,
and *Anjo negro*

BY

FRED M. CLARK

CHAPEL HILL

NORTH CAROLINA STUDIES IN THE ROMANCE
LANGUAGES AND LITERATURES
U.N.C. DEPARTMENT OF ROMANCE LANGUAGES

1991

Library of Congress Cataloging-in-Publication Data

Clark, Fred M.
  Impermanent structures: semiotic readings of Nelson Rodrigues' Vestido de noiva, Album de família, and Anjo negro / by Fred M. Clark.
  p. — cm. — (North Carolina studies in the Romance languages and literatures; no. 238)
  Includes bibliographical references.
  ISBN 0-8078-9242-4
  1. Rodrigues, Nelson. Vestido de noiva. 2. Rodrigues, Nelson. Album de família. 3. Rodrigues, Nelson. Anjo negro. 4. Theater-Semiotics. I. Title. II. Series.
PQ9697.R66V434   1991   91-19885
869.2–dc20   CIP

© 1991. Department of Romance Languages. The University of North Carolina at Chapel Hill.

ISBN 0-8078-9242-4

DEPÓSITO LEGAL: V. 1.553 - 1991   I.S.B.N. 84-401-2063-X
ARTES GRÁFICAS SOLER, S. A. - LA OLIVERETA, 28 - 46018 VALENCIA - 1991

for Murlin

CONTENTS

	Page
ACKNOWLEDGMENTS	11
I. INTRODUCTION: THE QUESTION OF TEXTS. APPROACHES. NELSON RODRIGUES AND THE BRAZILIAN THEATER	13
II. ICONIC, INDEXICAL, AND SYMBOLIC ASPECTS OF THE SIGN IN *VESTIDO DE NOIVA*	42
III. THE PHOTOGRAPHIC IMAGE AND THEATER: MISINTERPRETATION AND INTERPRETATION IN *ÁLBUM DE FAMÍLIA*	72
IV. THE FICTIVE WORLDS OF *ANJO NEGRO*	98
REFERENCES	124

ACKNOWLEDGMENTS

This book is the result of my studies and research in semiotics begun during the Fall of 1982 with Monica Rector, Visiting Professor of Semiotics at Indiana University for that term. During the same semester Professor Darlene Sadlier of the Department of Spanish and Portuguese invited me to give a lecture in a series she had organized entitled *New Directions in Brazilian Literary Studies*. I decided to apply the exciting new theories I was studying with Professor Rector to a play that for years had fascinated and intrigued me—Nelson Rodrigues' *Vestido de noiva*. I wish to thank Professor Rector and Professor Sadlier, both dear friends and colleagues, for having pushed me into preparing that first lecture, that led to other talks and papers in which I used semiotic theories to analyze different works by Nelson Rodrigues. I have reworked and elaborated some of these initial studies, and have incorporated others into what constitutes the present text. Chapters II and III have been developed from short talks that were published in *Approches de l'Opéra* and *Semiotics 1983*. Chapter IV appeared in a slightly altered version in Spanish in *Dispositio* 13, 33-35 (1988).

I wish to express my gratitude to Thomas A. Sebeok, who has given me the chance to work at the Research Center for Language and Semiotic Studies at Indiana University. He has been a true friend and colleague; he patiently listened to me when I encountered problems in the research, and helped me to understand a number of aspects of semiotic theory. The generous support of the University Research Council of the University of North Carolina has made possible the research and publication of this work.

The title was inspired by a passage from Patricia Waugh's brilliant work *Metafiction* (London and New York: Methuen, 1984).

The passage, in many ways, captures the essence of Nelson Rodrigues' theater:

> Contemporary metafictional writing is both a response and a contribution to an even more thoroughgoing sense that reality or history are provisional: no longer a world of eternal verities but a series of constructions, artifices, impermanent structures. (p. 7)

Fred M. Clark
University of North Carolina
Chapel Hill

CHAPTER I

INTRODUCTION: THE QUESTION OF TEXTS. APPROACHES. NELSON RODRIGUES AND THE BRAZILIAN THEATER

One of the most interesting but problematic areas of the semiotics of theater centers around the question of texts, specifically the antinomy of the closely interrelated performance and written texts (or as Elam [1980: 3] says, "that produced *in* the theater and that composed *for* the theater"). There are various theories among semioticians concerning the role of the written text in relation to the performance: some privilege the written text and see it as inscribing the performance signs (Serpieri 1978) or as a system of potential signs for performance (Gullí Pugliatti 1976); others see the written text and the performance as two autonomous phenomena, each of which must be considered as a separate entity in its own right (Helbo 1977; Ruffini 1978; De Marinis 1978; see also Bassnett-McGuire 1980: 50-51; Elam 1980: 3, and Feral 1982). Until recently, however, the written text has been the major focus of attention "both because of its permanence and accessibility and because, as a verbal structure, it was more open to investigation by such proven tools as those of discourse theory and narrative analysis" (Carlson 1985: 309).

Helbo, in examining the various semiotic theories concerning written and performance texts, points out that priority has been accorded the written text. Along the lines of the linguistic model, the written has often been viewed as the deep structure, and the performance as a variant of this:

> The double articulation textual framework/scenic level by which the text appears more or less as the invariant, as the deep structure, seems to validate the priority given that which is written. This priority was first expressed in theory of *simple implication* developed by Barthes who himself was inspired by Hjelmslev. The *simple implication* links a constant (a determining function)—in this case, a text which serves as the basis for a dramatization—with a variable (a determining function)—the re-presentation of this text. (Helbo 1977:173-174; cf. also Kuznicka 1986)

The problem is similar to one that has concerned literary scholars as they have attempted to define the literary text by distinguishing between literary and everyday discourse. In treating theater, however, the problem becomes more complicated: first a distinction between written and spoken discourse must be established, then a distinction must be drawn among literary, theatrical, and ordinary discourse.

Serpieri *et al.* (1981), in working with the segmentation of the dramatic text, have distinguished among the three in terms of a "third articulation" (the correlation of language and the pragmatic context):

> Theatrical language is distinguishable from "literary" language by such a "third articulation," becoming analogous to an utterance geared toward the speaking situation in everyday language, in that it produces meaning in relation to a pragmatic context. On the other hand, theatrical language is distinguishable from everyday discourse on the grounds that in the latter the deictic dimension does not need to be inscribed semantically within the verbal fabric of discourse itself, remaining a pure and simple *index*, while in the former the indexical dimension is semanticized, *becomes iconic* (being inscribed, with a surplus of information, within the verbal-pragmatic fabric) and *becomes symbolic* (entering into the paradigmatic axes of a text-action which, far from retaining the fragmentary or "spontaneous" character of a collection of everyday utterances, appears as an organic and "fictitious" structure). (1981: 165-166)

The nature of the problem of written text vs. performance is semiotic, and has been dealt with as such by Alter and Elam, who agree in their conclusion that what is involved is different signifying systems: a written language, usually analyzed by critics as a literary text, and a language of performance that has to be approached not only in terms of a literary code, but also in terms of other codes that are constitutive features of its composition.

While the written text consists of a purely linguistic code, its transformation into performance ("the performance is the synchronic confrontation of signifying systems, and it is their interaction, not their history, that is offered to the spectator and that produces meaning" Pavis [1988: 86]) involves both verbal and nonverbal systems:

> Whereas the script consists of verbal signs/letters only, the performance is composed of verbal as well as nonverbal signs (such as paralinguistic and kinesic signs, costumes, props, and stage settings). This means that, in a strict sense, they have no signs in common: the verbal signs in the written play appear as letters, and those in the staging as sounds. Thus, the script and the performance have to be seen as texts brought forth by means of two different semiotic systems—that of written language and that of the theater (consisting of spoken language and several nonverbal sign systems). (Fischer-Lichte 1987: 199)

As Alter (1981: 114) has said, "Total theater needs both text and performance"; Elam (1977: 140), following Barthes' (1972: 261-262) idea of theater as a "real informational polyphony" (i.e., the performance simultaneously emits a multiplicity of signs), says that it is only in the performance that theater can acquire its particular qualities of density and openness as the various codes converge and generate meaning. De Marinis (1987: 107) insists that to the polyphonic quality "we must add that the performance text or, more exactly, its dense signifying surface, is characterized by its *nondiscreteness* (in that it is continuous), its *instability* (in that it is variable), and its *impermanence* (in that it is ephemeral)."

In studies such as those in the present volume (as in the classroom where we teach drama and theater), we cannot depend on performance for analysis, so we must turn to the written word as our basis, keeping in mind the concept of total theater while wrestling with the idea of written text/performance (cf. Ubersfeld 1977, in which the French semiotician emphasizes that the written text may be analyzed to discover its signs of performability, signs that allow directors and actors to construct the meaningful sign the performance becomes). What we must constantly think of is not a specific performance, but rather the transformation of the script text into an ideal (or virtual) performance. Pagnini points out that the analysis of one specific performance as standing for a play's text is invalid because each play is a multiplicity of texts, the sum total of all its performances, which include individual and collective receptions. What remains in establishing a text for analysis is either a reconstruction of the play's historic reception or "a theatrical semiotics that does not take the semiosic processes of one particular performance as the object of description but describes the type of semiosic processes that make up the ideal theatrical performance, imagined in the completeness of its functions" (Pagnini 1987: 90). As Alter (1987: 43) has noted, "critics can and do recreate performances from memory, notes, or photographs, but, in so doing, they are making personal statements which must be taken on faith, at best as second-hand accounts of authentic impressions." These impressions are, as the critic says, inadequate for analysis, so "ultimately one must come back to the written text which alone allows for meaningful communication" (Alter 1987: 43; cf. De Marinis [1986: 1090], who points out that since the second half of the 1970s two schools of thought have developed among semioticians of theater: one in which the single performance is the object of analysis and one which emphasizes "theoretical, total, or partial approaches to the semiotic dynamics of the theatrical phenomenon"). However, when reading a play "[o]ne should always at least imagine a performance . . . even when dealing with playwrights like Ibsen or Strindberg, whose scripts seem to require us only to visualize people living in their homes, rather than actors performing on a stage" (Hornby 1986: 179). Perhaps the most sensible approach to the reading of the dramatic script as a theatrical work has been proposed by Chaudhuri; she speaks of a T-Text (Total Text), which is neither the written text nor the performance, but rather "*all* signs, from both verbal and nonverbal systems of signification, which the author includes directly or referentially in his script, and which he intends its production to employ" (1986: 32).

The question then arises: what are the irreducible elements of the written text that guarantee its recognition regardless of historical moment or interpreter. The point here is that there are constraints imposed on the performance by the written text (Issacharoff [1988a: 61] says that "Both the didascalia and the dialogue act as constraints on the virtual or on the ultimate performance"), and a director has neither freedom to ignore nor to follow too rigidly the instructions in the written text when turning it into a performance. As Hornby (1986: 179) perceptively notes, "As performance evolves in length and complexity, the need is apparent to everyone, including the performers themselves, to have a basic, controlling plan, which is what a script essentially is." There is, in other words, an intention in the written text, some idea that the playwright had when he composed the work of how it should be presented on the stage.

Johansen (1985: 256), in his work on semiotics and text interpretation, confronts the problem of intention and warns against the dangers of being accused of committing the error of "intentional fallacy"; he concludes, however, that since it is "impossible to understand the meaning of a text without determining its mode of enunciation, an analysis of intentions is a necessary prerequisite for text interpretation." By discussing intention, I do not mean to fall into the position of maintaining that the text is a repository of stable, unchanging meanings; there is, in my opinion, an intention in the text to "affect an audience" (Kirby 1987: xi) and to signify and communicate something through the signs of the text in a particular way. However, this intention is only one aspect on which new and multiple possible meanings may be constructed by the receiver. Johansen justifies his position by saying that "even the most casual conversation fulfills some purpose, perhaps nothing more than serving to establish contact, secure the lines of communication, and ensure social interaction. This means that in order to interpret a given text a semiotic text analysis ought to establish its purpose; and since purpose implies the conception of an end, the analysis ought to incorporate this as well" (1985: 256).

Elam (1988: 41), in his consideration of the pragmatics of drama and theater, approaches intentionality from the point of view of speech act theory, originally proposed by Austin and Searle. He points out that this analytic approach is the one most often used, and that one of its advantages for semiotics is that it considers "all of Morris's pragmatic factors—uses, users, and effects—in a single and hermetically sealed system." Elam (1988: 43) cautiously indicates that intention in the communicative act must be thought of in terms of two lines of communication existent in theater—the internal axis ("the fictional communication between the dramatis personae") and the external ("between dramatist and text [which] involves the intentionality or the force of the text itself as communicative act"). The two are, of course, intimately linked, but what is of interest to us here is the communication between dramatist and text, and what ultimately results in the confrontation between text and reader or spectator. Intentionality of an artistic text (as opposed to a political pamphlet, historical texts, didactic writings, etc.) is often more dependent upon the receiver than upon the text itself. However, as Schogt (1988: 56-58) points out, there are certain formal aspects (e.g., genre and special uses of language) that may be intentionally encoded into the text (Schogt uses poetry as an example of the artistic text; however, we may extract from his discussion certain points that are applicable to theater). The formal aspects are signs that have to do with how the play should be performed, and thus influence meanings that emerge during the spectacle. The signs are a part of the T-Text, as formulated by Chaudhuri (1986: 32), who says that "the dramatic significance of the play will be based on the proper inclusion of all the signs indicated by the T-Text."

At the same time, it must be noted that the constraints imposed by the written text and the lack of freedom afforded the °director in transforming the semiotic system of the written word to the semiotic systems of the performance include those that forbid him from following the written text so literally as to make it (or parts of it) incomprehensible to the present audience. Fischer-Lichte (1987: 210) has noted that alternative theatrical signs must be chosen if the intention of the text is to be preserved. A certain flexibility is needed, and even required, in following the playwright's instructions because "[t]hese directions are provided on the basis of a particular theatrical code generally accepted at the time the play was written. Since such codes are historically determined, if these instructions are actually followed on the contemporary stage, meanings as well as effects could be brought forth that are quite opposite to those intended." Although he recognizes that the printed text is far from being "the whole of the drama", Esslin concedes a permanence in the written text as opposed to the ephemeral signifiers of the performance, and adds that it is the more permanent form that allows for a certain flexibility in conveying meaning through the performance:

> For it [the permanence of the written text] allows those texts to be re-incarnated in a very wide variety of different performances

in different environments and different epochs, and thus makes them flexible enough to be relatively easily adjusted to successive historical, cultural and technological conditions and to remain viable over several centuries. (1987: 80)

Some critics and scholars have discussed this aspect of the written text—i.e., the author's directives or instructions, which form an integral part of the text—and the director's responsibility in following these. Elam (1988: 45) essentially agrees with Fischer-Lichte in that there must be some flexibility accorded the director in terms of the playwright's instructions, but refers to these as "pseudonarrative information"; he says that "any director worth a directorial chair will tend to take the author's directions—if you will excuse the lexical pileup—not as directive but as so much pseudonarrative information that can be used or discarded according to need. What remains is the fictional doing, or dialogue."

Magaldi, in discussing the performances of Nelson Rodrigues' texts, also rejects the notion of following to the letter the instructions of the written text; for him, the performance is a process of construction based on a dialogue between the director and the written text, and from this dialogue emerge aspects of the work which even the author did not imagine:

> Toda montagem é uma leitura pessoal. O encenador sensível traz à tona, freqüentemente, valores insuspeitados pelo próprio dramaturgo. A obra contém elementos latentes, inexpressos pelo diálogo, que o artista inteligente capta e materializa. Além dos outros elementos que o compõem, o espetáculo é perfeito quando as concepções do dramaturgo e do diretor se harmonizam e atingem plenitude. A encenação que simplesmente seguisse as sugestões óbvias do texto o desserviria por completo. O diretor pode não observar uma rubrica, se ela não é essencial para a organicidade do texto e seu propósito foi o de alcançar outro efeito, indispensável para a imagem do conjunto. (Magaldi 1987: 82)

> [Every staging is a personal reading. The sensitive director frequently brings to the surface values unsuspected by the dramatist himself. The work contains latent elements, unexpressed by the dialogue, which the intelligent artist captures and materializes. Besides the other elements that constitute it, the spectacle is perfect when the conceptions of the dramatist and the director

are in harmony and attain completeness. The staging that simply follows the obvious suggestions of the text does a complete disservice to it. The director can disregard the written stage directions, if they are not essential to the organicity of the text and if his objective is that of obtaining another effect that was indispensable to the image of the whole.]

The question of the written text and performance also leads to another question which has been the focus of study of literary texts, and more recently of theatrical works—that of reader (in the case of theater, reader/spectator) reception and response. Since the written text and the performance reach the perceiver through different signifying systems, it stands to reason that receptive processes and response to each are different. Both texts are signs that mediate between a perceiver and an object, but in the case of the performance there is an interference that occurs in the form of director and actors who interpret for themselves and reinterpret for the audience, adding to the written text all that is missing in concrete terms—i.e., voice, gestures, movements, physical space and setting, etc. In both cases, the perceiver is, of course, conditioned to receive the text in different manners; there are codes and conventions that govern each text, and these will influence the reader's or spectator's reception. For example, a person may be quite accustomed to reading novels and short stories, and thus will read the play text in much the same manner; or the person may be quite acquainted with theater, and will read the text in a more "theatrical" manner. Likewise, one spectator may be more familiar with theatrical codes and conventions than another spectator who thus cannot participate as fully in the experience of the performance. In the case of the theater, there has been little headway made in establishing a semiotic model of spectator response. De Marinis (1985: 6) has pointed out that the study of spectator response and esthetics of theatrical reception "must consist of a cognitive semiotic of theatrical comprehension, or better and more broadly, of the experience of the spectator (also cf. Chaudhuri 1984, Coppieters 1981, De Marinis 1983, De Toro 1987: 129-164, Pavis 1985, and Helbo 1987; for an overview of response and reception theories in general cf. Holub 1984). Any such approach necessarily makes the spectator an accomplice in the production of the text—i.e., the meaning of the performance only emerges when it is perceived by a spectator, when he enters into a constructive dialogue or participation with that which occurs in the stage space. And what occurs in that space is the result of the efforts of various participants—dramatist, director, actors.

De Marinis (1987: 101), in his definition of a dramaturgy of the spectator, describes the spectator's participation in the performance in terms of various operations/actions which include "perception, interpretation, aesthetic appreciation, memorization, emotive and intellectual response, etc." He concludes that "it is only through these actions that the performance text achieves its fullness, becoming realized in all its semantic and communicative potential." The notion of the performance achieving a fullness of potential only makes sense in terms of De Marinis' "model spectator" ("a hypothetical construct and . . . simply a part of a theoretical metalanguage" [1987: 102]). Fullness implies the notion of completeness, and this seems arbitrary in terms of the empirical spectator; the sense of fullness would vary from one spectator to another in the same performance, and even for the same spectator from one performance to another, since the text is not a stable, set source of meanings.

This points to another interesting aspect of the performance (already applied to literary texts) which has been touched upon (but not elaborated) recently by semioticians of theater: the performance as a deconstructionist activity. In the case of the ephemeral performance text, which varies from one staging to the next and from one day to the next in a run, the fact that the text is not a repository of fixed and invariable meanings is perhaps more obvious because of its immediacy and dynamism than with the novel or short story (which, of course, varies from one reading to the next). The performance, as Issacharoff (1988b: 139) says, undermines the notion of the written text, the "logocentric" text as forever the same stable and meaningful unit. The deconstructionist view would insist instead on the written text opening itself up to new and different meanings as interpretations—on the part of directors, actors, and audience—merge and forge new and, at the same time, *unstable* meanings with each performance. Each performance thus is seen as a one-time, fleeting and fragile experience that can never be duplicated in its totality in another performance (and another performance excludes a videotaped performance, which is *not* theater but rather a taping of theater). As Pavis (who has worked with the notion of text, performance, reception, and social context) indicates, it is not only the performance text that produces multiple readings, but also the dramatic text:

> The text, that of the script or the performance, can only be understood intertextually, when confronted with the discursive and ideological structures of a period or of a corpus of texts. The dramatic and the performance texts must be considered in relation to the *Social Context*—that is, other texts and discourses about reality produced by a society. This relationship being the most fragile and variable imaginable, the same dramatic text readily produces an infinite number of readings. (Pavis 1988: 93-94)

However, while maintaining that both texts are open to a number of possible interpretations and meanings, Pavis still points out that a work does not present an "infinite number of amorphous possibilities; rather, it assumes meanings which are historically differentiated according to changes in the Social Context" (1987: 128).

Theoreticians recently have approached a solution to the problem of the written text/performance text dichotomy by abandoning the purely linguistic model of the sign proposed by Saussure (signifier [the sign-vehicle] + signified [the mental concept produced by the signifier] = signification) and turning to Peirce's notion of the sign as a triadic structure that takes into account not only signifier and signified, but also the idea of object or referent. Peirce's sign consists of a sign vehicle (the sign, the sign in itself, or *representamen*; cf. Buczynska-Garewicz's [1981: 189-190] discussion of the confusion that arises over Peirce's use of the term "sign" for total triadic structure and for the vehicle of meaning), the object (referent), and the intepretant (the sign which interprets the sign; "the interpreting thought"—MS 493: 2). As Peirce (CP 8.343) says

> I define a *Sign* as anything which on the one hand is so determined by an Object and on the other hand so determines an idea in a person's mind, that this latter determination, which I term the *Interpretant* of the sign, is thereby mediately determined by that Object. A sign, therefore, has a triadic relation to its Object and to its Interpretant.

The American logician's semiotic (an elaborate complex of various phenomenological categories and trichotomies which will be explained in more detail as needed throughout the chapters in which the individual plays are analyzed) is essentially a "theory of experience, a theory of consciousness" (Zeman 1977a: 241-242). It expounds a dynamic process of sign production, thus of perception; this accommodates well theater analysis, which must be always aware of a number of signs and codes operative and producing meaning at any given moment of the text.

Pavis (1981, 1982), Elam (1980), and Pladott (1982) have found the application of Peirce's theory to the theatrical sign to yield positive results; as Pladott (1982: 31) has noted, an added advantage is that Peirce's model allows the semiotician to avoid "such unnecessary antinomies as written text/performance; illusionistic/nonillusionistic theatre, etc." By this, I assume that the critic has in mind the fact that the reader of the text will create in his mind the same type of signs that would exist on stage in a performance—i.e., the signs would be either iconic, indexical, or symbolic (this trichotomy of signs is based on the relation—similarity, contiguity, or convention—between the sign vehicle and the object). As Pavis (1981: 88) notes, the icon-index-symbol distinction "does not divide performance into text and stage . . . on the contrary, it regroups, in every category, signs that could equally belong in both domains." Of course, all language is symbolic, and the written text (considered a literary text by many critics) is made up of symbols; but symbols, as Johansen (1986a: 114) says, "in order to be meaningful . . . must have icons and indices attached to them." He quotes Peirce's definition of an assertion to make his point:

> . . . an assertion is an *act* which represents that an icon represents the objects of an index. Thus, in the assertion, 'Mary is redheaded', 'red-headed' is not an icon itself, it is true, but a symbol. But its interpretant is an icon, a sort of composite photograph of all the red-headed persons one has seen. 'Mary' in like manner, is interpreted by a sort of composite memory of all the occasions which forced my attention upon that girl. The putting of these together makes another *index* which has a force tending to make the icon an index of Mary. (L75, Carnegie Institution Correspondence, 1902, L75D ISP 323)

The director can (and often must) vary the sign vehicle, but the type of sign created by reading the written text and the type that emerges in the performance would be essentially the same. For example, if in the written text there is the mention of a table, and the table is simply that—i.e., it does not go beyond the iconic and indexical—it should be the same on the stage. However, if it is obvious within the written text that the table is symbolic of something other than itself (perhaps it is symbolic of a sacrificial altar), then on the stage it must also be a symbolic sign. Of course, the director can portray this visually in any number of ways, but the sign function must remain the same from written text to performance.

It is interesting and pertinent to note here that, in reference to the question of written texts and performance text, Fischer-Lichte (1987: 203) has formulated her notion of the relationship of the two in terms of Peirce's definition of the sign: "[T]he theatrical signs of acting may function as interpretants of the drama's verbal signs (an interpretant is defined as any 'representamen which is determined by another representamen'." Both texts are signs, but they are neither the *same* sign nor totally equivalent signs, since they are not from the same system. The interpretant sign (the performance) is determined by another sign (the written text). Fischer-Lichte adheres to the Peircean notion that the interpretant is "a more developed sign"; the performance, in other words, is a more complete realization than the written text because in the transformation various sign systems converge as written letters on a page become visual and auditory—i.e., as ostension takes the place of description (cf. Eco 1977: 110; Elam 1980: 30).

The present study will examine three plays by the Brazilian dramatist Nelson Rodrigues (1912-1980) in light of various theories of theater, with an emphasis on the semiotics (particularly Peircean) of theater. Nelson (as he is often referred to by critics) is one of the dramatists who brought Brazilian dramaturgy into the twentieth century with his innovative, avant-garde text *Vestido de noiva* in 1943 (cf. Lins 1975: 63: "Um motivo do sucesso da peça de Nelson Rodrigues está na sua integração nas modernas correntes de teatro" [One reason for the success of Nelson Rodrigues' play is its integration into the modern trends of theater]). *Modernismo* (the Modernist Movement) as manifested in the Semana de Arte Moderna [The Week of Modern Art] of 1922 had as one of its basic tenets the modernization of the arts (both auditory and visual) and letters into a more accurate reflection and representation of contemporary Brazilian realities. However, despite the tremendous achievements in music, the graphic arts, and poetry, *Modernismo* effected few changes in drama and theater of the 1920s or 1930s. Theater continued under the influence of the nineteenth-century canons and conventions, or as Prado has summarized these, "os três pilares básicos da cultura official brasileira em matéria de teatro: a ópera, as temporadas francesas e as companhias vindas de Portugal" (1975: 140) [the three basic pillars of official Brazilian culture in terms of theater: the opera, the season of French productions, and the visiting companies from Portugal]. There was, in other words, little in the way of artistic modernization in terms of a Brazilian theater; the Brazilian theatrical scene was still dominated, in many senses, by foreign influences. These influences, however, were not those of the vanguard; they were nineteenth-century influences that had become static and were stifling the development of Brazilian theater.

Prado (1968: 25-26) has portrayed the Brazilian theatrical scene of the first decades of the twentieth century in these terms:

> A onda de teatro musicado, ao se retirar, depois de tocada a última valsa da última opereta vienense, deixou o nosso teatro dramático mais pobre e vazio do que nunca, sem público, sem autores, e até sem atores de drama ou comédia. Cortadas as amarras com a vanguarda literária de Europa, estabelecidas mal e mal pelo Realismo, permanecemos à margem de toda a revolução estética de fins do século dezenove e princípios deste. Stanislawski, Gordon Craig, Copeau, são influências que não chegaram nem sequer a atravessar o oceano. Mais uma vez tivemos de recomeçar do início, por onde o nosso teatro sempre recomeça: pela comediazinha de costumes, de âmbito puramente local, a exemplo de Martins Pena.
>
> [The wave of musical theater, upon withdrawing when the last waltz from the last Viennese operetta was played, left our dramatic theater poorer and more empty than ever, without public, without authors, and even without dramatic or comedic actors. The bonds with the European literary vanguard—poorly established by Realism—were cut, and we remained on the margins of the entire esthetic revolution of the end of the nineteenth and the beginning of the twentieth century. Stanislavski, Gordon Craig, Copeau are influences that did not arrive, nor even crossed the ocean. Once again we had to start over from the beginning, from where our theater always re-begins: with the

little comedy of customs, of a purely local ambit, as in the case of Martins Pena.]

A few innovative texts, such as Oswald de Andrade's *O homem e o cavalo, O rei da vela,* and *A morta* were written in the 1930s, but these were not performed.

Oswald de Andrades' plays were relegated to the printed page for decades, and thus did not have an immediate impact on the theater (as Prado [1975: 139-40] has said of Oswald's texts, "O espírito da Semana, se não propriamente a sua realização, forneceu aos nossos palcos pelo menos um autor" [The spirit of the Week, if not its effect, furnished our stage with at least an author]). The lack of performance was due to two factors that inhibited any type of innovative change in the theater at the time: political censorship and the fact that there simply did not exist in Brazil at that moment the talent or the resources for the production of such revolutionary and innovative texts (cf. Magaldi 1967: 7). These conditions persisted until the 1940s, specifically 1943, when the felicitous encounter of an avant-garde text by a young writer who was more versed in journalism than theater, and an innovative emigré director (the Polish director Ziembinski) who could take advantage of the local resources and talent, produced what would become a landmark in Brazilian dramaturgy–the production of *Vestido de noiva* on December 28, 1943, in the Teatro Municipal do Rio de Janeiro by the amateur group Os Comediantes. And it is important here to note the importance of amateur theatrical groups in Brazil at the time. They were the centers of experimentation and innovation in the theater. As Prado (1968: 29) has noted: "A bandeira da renovação foi desfraldada de início pelos amadores, pelo Teatro do Estudante, de Pascoal Carlos Magno, e Os Comediantes, de Santa Rosa, no Rio de Janeiro; em São Paulo, através do Grupo de Teatro Experimental, semente de onde brotaria a Escola de Arte Dramática, considerada com justiça a melhor do País, e pelo Teatro de Amadores de Pernambuco, de Waldemar de Oliveira, em Recife." [The flag of renovation was unfurled in the beginning by the amateurs, by the Student Theater of Pascoal Carlos Magno, and The Comedians, of Santa Rosa, in Rio de Janeiro; in São Paulo, through the Group of Experimental Theater, from which the School of Dramatic Art, justly considered the best in the country would originate, and by the Amateur Theater of Pernambuco, of Waldemar de Oliveira, in Recife].

Lins (1975: 62) believes that Nelson's play could never have achieved such a success without the collaboration of Ziembinski and Santa Rosa (the scenographer) who contributed those elements that exist beyond the written text; without this collaboration, the text would have remained simply a work of literature (like the texts of Oswald de Andrade): "Pois o que caracteriza o teatro é a fusão da arte literária com a arte da arquitetura cênica. Faz-se o teatro com o autor, o ator, o público, o diretor, o cenógrafo, e mais o ritmo, as cores, a música, toda uma arquitetura cênica, todo um conjunto de condições que constitui exatamente o espetáculo" [What characterizes the theater is the fusion of literary art with the art of scenic construction. Theater is made with the author, the actor, the director, the scenographer, in addition to the rhythm, the colors, the music, an entire scenic construction, an entire combination of conditions that precisely constitute the spectacle].

With the performance of *Vestido de noiva*, the tension that guarantees progress and evolution in all the arts was confirmed—i.e., the conflict between the old and the new, the stagnant and the innovative. The static state of Brazilian drama was threatened by Nelson's dynamic, innovative text, which opened the door to innovations in all aspects of theater—text, staging, directing, acting, etc. The theater in Brazil, however (as is generally the case in any country), did not immediately undergo a total reformation. On the contrary, the conflict between the new style and the old persisted for years, with the new opening paths for young, talented dramatists who experimented with theatrical techniques while exploring Brazilian and universal realities (e.g., Jorge Andrade, Ariano Suassuna, Gianfrancesco Guarnieri, Dias Gomes, Augusto Boal, Plínio Marcos, and a host of younger writers in the 1970s and 1980s). Ziembinski (1975: 56), who was so instrumental in the modernization of the Brazilian stage, describes what began with the production of *Vestido de noiva*:

> Um novo estilo foi então implantado. Digo isto sem nenhuma modéstia, e sem vontade de jogar confete em cima de nós. Mas conosco nasceu uma nova técnica que durante anos iria lutar com aquilo que já estava composto. Nós não queríamos guerra. Queríamos chamar as pessoas para um trabalho junto. Mas a guerra foi declarada por parte daqueles que estavam acomodados a um certo tipo de espectáculo. Fomos chamados de aventurei-

ros, de gente sem ética que queria derrubar aquilo que já existia, propondo de uma maneira quase quixotesca as coisas que nunca seriam aceitas pelo público. Graças a Deus foram aceitas. E até hoje estão presentes no moderno teatro brasileiro.

[A new style was then implanted. I say this without any modesty and without wanting to flatter us. But with us there was born a new technique that for years was going to conflict with that which was already in place. We did not want to fight. We wanted to call people to work together. But war was declared by those who were accustomed to a certain type of spectacle. We were called adventurers, people without ethics, who wanted to destroy that which already existed by proposing in an almost quixotic manner things that would never be accepted by the public. Thank goodness they were accepted. And even today they are present in the modern Brazilian theater.]

Although he continued in the profession of journalism, Nelson Rodrigues, over the next thirty-seven years, would exercise a strong and often polemical presence in the Brazilian theater.

Nelson was loved and hated by the critics, who praised his innovations but condemned his content, which they considered obscene and pornographic. As Nelson himself notes in his *O reacionário. Memórias e confissões* (1977a: 314-15):

E, de fato, eu era um ser polêmico. Imaginem vocês um centauro que fosse a metade cavalo e a outra metade também. Era esta a minha imagem para gregos e troianos. Detestado por uns, tarado para outros, mal-amado por todos.

Dirão vocês que exagero. Mas creiam que durante vinte anos, fui eu o único autor obsceno do teatro brasileiro. Na estréia da minha peça *Anjo negro*, o *Diário da Noite* me chamou de *tarado*, no alto de página, em oito colunas. . .

. . . Havia em torno de minha pessoa, textos e atos, uma sólida e crudelíssima unanimidade.

[And, in fact, I was a polemical being. Imagine a centaur that was half horse and the other half also. That was my image to both sides. Hated by some, degenerate to others, disliked by all.

You will say that I am exaggerating. But believe me when I say that for twenty years, I was the only obscene author of the Brazilian theater. On the opening of my play *Anjo negro*, the newspaper *Diário da Noite* called me a *degenerate*, at the top of the page, across eight columns.

. . . There was a solid and cruel unanimity surrounding my person, texts, and acts.]

As Prado (1988: 130-31) points out, Nelson fell out of favor because of his support of the military regime in 1964. However, he was rediscovered in the late seventies by the director Antunes Filho, who, fascinated by the playwright's originality, set about to rescue him from "a inscrição . . . no gênero da comédia de costumes" (Magaldi 1987: 166) [the inscription . . . into the genre of comedy of manners]. Antunes Filho's careful readings and productions of Nelson's texts have received critical acclaim in Brazil and abroad (cf. Magaldi 1987: 168-88). His success confirms the fact that Nelson's texts have maintained their sense of innovation and modernity, both on the thematical and technical levels: "Se o autor de *Vestido de noiva*, mais de quarenta anos após a estréia da peça, continua a parecer para a maioria dos críticos e dos encenadores o mais atual dramaturgo brasileiro é certamente porque foi, entre todos, o que mais ousou, desafiando ao mesmo tempo a moral, a lógica e o decoro artístico" (Prado 1988: 136) [If the author of *Vestido de noiva*, more than forty years after the opening of the play, continues to appear to the majority of critics and directors to be the most current Brazilian dramatist, it is certainly because he, among all of them, is the one who was the most daring, defying all at once morals, logic, and artistic decorum].

Although each is a highly innovative and polished work in itself, the texts analyzed in this study share a number of common elements that characterize Nelson's plays of the 1940s. These common traits are also discernible under different guises in the plays that constitute what some critics see as a second phase in the playwright's theatrical production: namely, those dramas written beginning with *A falecida* (1953) and referred to as the "comédias humanas" [human comedies] (cf. Pelegrino 1966: 9-13). As will be seen in the individual chapters, a central preoccupation of Nelson's is the antinomy between reality and illusion in human existence, and how the individual copes with what is often a merging and confusion of what should normally constitute separate and defineable poles. Most basic to Nelson's production of the 1940s and early 1950s is his artistic formulation of a highly original portrayal and response to reality–

both his concept of personal reality and the collective reality of the Brazilian theater of his epoch. His texts, in a certain sense, become a personal space in which the author exhibits his own struggle with the complex realities of a world in which he never felt totally at ease: ". . . já disse, sem nenhuma piada, que sou uma alma da *belle epoque*. Não gosto da minha época, não tenho afinidades com ela. A meu ver, estamos assistindo ao fracasso do ser humano. Isso não quer dizer que mais adiante ele não se levante, mas no momento o ser humano está de quatro" (Rodrigues 1977b: v) [I have already said, without joking, that I am a soul from the *belle époque*. I don't like my epoch, I don't feel any affinities to it. As I see it, we are witnessing the failure of the human being. That doesn't mean that later he will not rise up, but at the moment the human being is on all fours].

At the same time, Nelson Rodrigues is representative of the twentieth century in the manner in which he deals with reality in his works: he uses the element of fantasy (and what is theater essentially if not a treatment of reality through fantasy?) to portray the human being caught in an eternal search for absolutes and meaning, and he uses the fantastic in the techniques he employs on the stage to capture the human condition. Here I accept Hume's (1984: xii) definition of fantasy—"the deliberate departure from the limits of what is usually accepted as real and normal"—and her assumption that such a departure from reality does not preclude comment upon it. On the contrary, the departure from what is "real and normal" in Nelson's texts constitutes an extraordinary comment in the form of questioning reality and concluding that it is ambivalent and arbitrary. In the texts written in the 1940s and early 1950s, Nelson incorporates a number of elements that would not be considered real and normal (particularly in the Brazilian theater of the time). In *Vestido de noiva*, for example, the entire stage represents throughout a large portion of the spectacle the workings of a mind in the final moments of life, reliving the past and also living out fantasies; spatial and temporal boundaries are eliminated as past and present, living and dead, real and unreal cohabit the stage space. *Valsa No. 6* (1951), which Magaldi (1981a) includes among the psychological plays, presents a similar situation, except that the element of fantasy is extended to include a dead protagonist who relives important moments of her life as she attempts to understand who she is, where she is, and why she is there. The text has one character who engages in a long monologue in which she creates characters and events—as well as time and space—through verbal and nonverbal (gestures, movements, etc.) signs. Two of the plays under study here—*Anjo negro*, *Álbum de família*—belong to the "peças míticas" [mythic plays] of Nelson's theatrical production. These are characterized by personages who belong more to the realm of myth and fantasy than to a concrete, identifiable setting peopled by living beings. They are more symbolic abstractions or structures involved in timeless, eternal struggles, which become signs of the dichotomy between the real and the illusory. *A falecida* (1953), bridges the mythic and the human phases as well as combining elements of the pyschological and the mythic; it is what Nelson labeled his "tragédia carioca" [cariocan tragedy]. It presents more everyday beings in more human situations. However, even here Nelson fuses—in a highly visual manner—the elements of fantasy and the real as the actors themselves construct the settings through a minimum of scenic metonymy and through pantomimic movements and gestures.

Nelson's response to the Brazilian stage of his day through his own texts was, to a great extent, a response to the age-old question of realism and verisimilitude. *Vestido de noiva* was written and performed at a time when established conventions of realism and the portrayal of reality in the arts had already been questioned and challenged in painting and prose (traditional canons of poetry and music, dating from the same period of the nineteenth century, had also been subverted during the 1920s with the Modernists). And prose fiction—with writers such as Guimarães Rosa, Clarice Lispector, and Lêdo Ivo—was about to enter a new phase that would correspond even more closely to what Nelson would achieve in his plays in the 1940s—i.e., the questioning in subtle ways of the conventions that define realism and verisimilitude and the negation of these as the artist creates his own personal concept of presenting an illusion of reality on the stage.

Nelson overcomes the mimetic prejudices of the Brazilian theater of his day (as well as those of the novel as reflected in the novel of the Northeast) and creates a work in which the reality of the work itself—i.e., the inner structures and principles that govern its construction—is revealed. The work is then seen as a parallel or presentation in miniature of the extratextual world and the complex relations and interrelations of its existence rather than as a world separated and alienated from that reality. Art is, in other words, held up as a mirror of the world, but the image that emerges is not one that is constructed according to the principles of nineteenth-century realism. On the contrary, it presents an image of the world constructed according to conventions that correspond more to its epoch—an epoch molded by international conflicts, the advance of technology, the dissolution of traditional values (both social and artistic), and the questioning of human existence in general. Nelson captures these realities in his plays by establishing a concept of the real which is seen as defineable only in terms of contrast and conflict with the fantastic and the imaginary, and which often incorporates elements of these. The disintegrating mind of *Vestido de noiva* and the mythic worlds of *Anjo negro*, *Álbum de família* are perfect examples of fictional spaces in which such a fusion may take place and maintain (or construct) in a verisimilar manner a sense of realism.

Hume (1984), in discussing how fantasy is used in literature, distinguishes four possible types of literary response to reality: 1) literature of illusion, 2) expressive literature, 3) literature of revision, and 4) literature of disillusion. Literature of illusion, or escapist literature, includes such genres as the pastoral, the tale of conquest, the detective story, etc., and is characterized by an authorial attitude that reality cannot be changed, so the author "offers to disengage us from its grey unpleasantness and to enfold us in comforting illusions" (Hume 1984: 55). Nelson Rodrigues clearly finds reality to be unpleasant, but his texts, although dealing in fantasy at times, do not create pleasing alternative worlds that offer the spectator moments of reprieve from reality. The disagreeable aspects of humanity are consciously portrayed in his plays through the strong characters he creates and places in violent situations (generally this is verbal violence; physical violence is usually suggested rather than physically performed on stage).

In his memoirs, Nelson's (1977a) displeasure takes the form of more direct statements, without the artistic subtlety of the dramatic text that transforms these into themes. For example, he comments on dehumanization caused by the separation of love and sex ("O homem começou a própria desumanização quando separou o sexo do amor"-p. 370 [Man began his own dehumanization when he separated sex from love]), the lack of conscience in modern man (". . . o nosso mundo não está interessado na consciência humana"-p. 361 [. . . our world is not interested in the human conscience]), the difficulty in the modern world of separating the sane from the insane ("... em nossa época, o homem normal não é dessemelhante do insano. Ou os dois são loucos ou os dois são normais"–p. 360 [... in our epoch, the normal man is not unlike the insane man. Either the two are crazy or the two are normal]), the lack of communication among human beings ("... ninguém ouve ninguém .... O que chamamos diálogo é, na maioria dos casos, um monólogo, cuja resposta é outro monólogo. Por isso, a nossa vida é a busca desesperada de um ouvinte"–p. 330 [... nobody listens to anybody else .... What we call a dialogue is, in the majority of cases, another monologue. Because of that, our life is a desperate search for a listener]), the lack of family intimacy and closeness and values ("No passado, a nossa virtude ou nossa abjeção era enterrada no mistério de quatro paredes. Por exemplo:–a família. No bom tempo a família tinha intimidades invioláveis. Fazia-se o diabo dentro de um lar, com a prévia certeza de um sigilo total"–p. 286 [In the past, our goodness and our baseness were buried in the mystery of four walls. For example:–the family. You could do what the devil you wanted in your own home, and with the prior certainty of total secrecy]), the general fragility and weakness in the human being ("... aprendi a olhar no fundo da nossa brutal e indefesa fragilidade"–pp. 182-183 [... I learned to look into the depths of our brutal and helpless fragility]), and the notion of man as a prefabricated being who does not make choices ("Quanto à 'opção', não sei se ela existe. A meu ver, nunca optamos tão pouco. Somos pré-fabricados. É difícil para o homem moderno ousar um movimento próprio. Nossa vida é a soma de idéias feitas, de frases feitas, de sentimentos feitos, de atos feitos, de ódios feitos, de angústia feita"–p. 153 [As far as choice is concerned, I don't know if it exists. In my opinion, we have chosen so little. We are prefabricated. It is difficult for modern man to dare a movement on his own. Our lives are the sum of ready-made ideas, phrases, feelings, acts, hatreds, and ready-made anxiety]), and on the fact that mystery is removed even from death ("Nada pior, porém, do que a morte datada, que não admite uma dúvida, um suspense, uma esperança"–p. 375 [There is nothing worse, however, than a foreseen death that does not allow even a doubt, a bit of suspense, a hope]).

Even with the displeasure that he finds in existence and the human being in general, Nelson does not use his texts to create an escape or to create comforting illusions for his spectator. On the contrary, he portrays the unpleasant; as he states in defining his "teatro desagradável" [unpleasant theater], his plays are fetid and should awaken in the spectator a feeling or sense akin to typhoid, which corresponds to the unpleasantness of reality (Rodrigues 1949). It would seem that the negative and pessimistic aspects of Nelson's theater approximate his work more to the category of literature of disillusion (cf. Hume 1984: 124-143), which considers reality to be unknowable. Authors using this mode of literary response to reality "insist that our perception of reality is a function of perspective and vantage point" (Hume 1984: xiv). The limitations and unreliability of the senses, the variation of perceptions and interpretation of reality from one individual to another, and the limitations and constraints of language and communication are topics that characterize this type of writing and, to a certain extent, characterize those of Nelson's theatrical texts under study here. However, the one great difference between Nelson's and the works generally classified as literature of disillusion is that the Brazilian playwright never totally negates the human being (total negation in itself would constitute something much too absolute and without ambiguity for Nelson). On the contrary, he constantly portrays mankind as struggling to know and define his reality. There is no espousal of abdication of responsibility or of simply giving up and recognizing the futility of the struggle. Nelson's characters are trapped individuals who, perhaps, according to his statements about choice, cannot choose or go beyond their traps. However, even here the playwright is ambiguous–the human being is entrapped, and this trap seems inescapable, yet his characters strive for freedom, which comes through knowledge of reality, an ordering of the chaos that surrounds them. Nelson's work is not characterized by a lack of a program of action as are works of disillusion; his program of action, although carefully woven into the texts and not always obvious, is that to live is to strive constantly to know and order and find (or create) meaning.

Nelson's theater, I believe, contains more traits of expressive literature or the literature of vision (cf. Hume 1984: 82-101), which unlike escapist literature, does not reject everyday reality, and unlike literature of disillusion does not totally reject reality as unknowable. On the contrary, his plays take this reality and create from it new visions or perspectives for the reader to consider. As Hume says (1984: 56), "Literature of vision aims to disturb us by dislodging us from our settled sense of reality, and tries to engage our emotions on behalf of the new vision of the real." Nelson's plays, to a great extent, fall into this category of literary responses to reality. His stage becomes a space in which common reality is transformed into new (or defamiliarized) perspectives for the spectator; these perspectives, which are often unpleasant and discomfiting, simultaneously engage him and force him, at the same time, to rethink and reexamine his own realities, both internal and external. The everyday experiences of characters attempting to understand the signs that compose reality is simply foregrounded into exaggerated situations that range from the deep recesses of the individual conscious in the psychological plays to the primitive levels of the collective unconscious in the mythic plays (cf. Clark and García for analysis of Nelson's plays from these particular angles).

Literature of revision, in which the author attempts to change present reality in order to shape the future, presents certain characteristics that also may be seen in Nelson's theater. However, even with his moralizing strain and the sense of nostalgia for a past in which values were different and more defined, his works do not fall totally within the realm of this type, which is also referred to as didactic literature and can take the form of mythic narratives. His plays, like most literary works, contain a certain didactic element; the plays, however, tend more to disturb and upset whereas didactic literature tends "to offer the eventual comfort of order, of a program, of decisions made and laid down. It offers us the emotional pleasures of absolutes" (Hume 1984: 56). Critical thought on the part of the reader or spectator is not an aspect of the program of this type of literature; on the contrary, Nelson, although he wants his spectator to live the frightful, emotional experiences of his characters at the time of performance, believes that a moment of reflection and thought in which a critical attitude is formed must exist. This moment begins after the performance has ended; but during the stage life of the play, there is no distance (at least, not in the Brechtian sense) between spectator and characters: "Não há distância. O espectador subiu ao palco e não tem a noção da própria identidade. Está ali como o homem. E depois, quando acaba tudo, e só então, é que se faz a 'distância crítica'. A grande vida da boa peça só começa quando baixa o pano. É o momento de fazer a nossa meditação sobre o amor e a morte" (Rodrigues 1977a: 147-148) [There is no distance. The spectator goes onto the stage and has no notion of his own identity. He is there as a man. And then, when all is finished, and only then, can the critical distance be made. The great life of a good play only begins when the curtain goes down. It is the moment of our meditating on life and death]. This critical thought necessarily will include some meditation on reality. As the spectator ponders and attempts to draw specific conclusions concerning realities within the text and then to see how these pertain to his own extratextual reality, confusion reigns and no absolute, concrete conclusions can be drawn. For example, how many of Alaide's (*Vestido de noiva*) memories are accurate? Indeed, can the individual really relive a life in the final moments before death?

Among the common elements that characterize Nelson's plays, perhaps the most obvious include the innovative spirit in theme and technique, the extreme theatrical quality which ultimately manifests itself in the metatheatrical element, and the fact that the works often structure the spectator into the basic fabric of the text, creating a new relationship between stage and audience. The spirit of innovation is generally manifested in each text by at least one device that immediately grabs the attention of the spectator. From this device the playwright then generally proceeds to subvert audience expectations of theater and present his themes from an unusual—defamiliarized—perspective that allows for new interpretations of reality in both life and art. In *Vestido de noiva*, it is the unusual use of lighting on a highly stylized, divided stage; in *Anjo negro* it is the obvious use of the contrast and subversion of the traditional symbolism of black and white effected not only through costumes and stage props, but also through the use of black and white characters; in *Álbum de família*, it is the use of the notion of photography and the negation of the usual interpretations of the meaning of the photograph. These devices are usually turned into metatheatrical devices which, as Waugh says of metafiction, not only offer the spectator a better understanding of the fundamental theatrical structures, but also offer "extremely accurate models for understanding the contemporary experience of the world as a construction, an artifice, a web of interdependent semiotic systems" (1984: 9).

One of the most outstanding features of Nelson Rodrigues' theater is the metatheatrical quality that underlines and defines the texts to a certain extent (cf. Anspach 1987). Because of this feature, Nelson's stage in many ways resembles the avant-garde stage as characterized by Chaudhuri:

> Upon the denial of traditional aesthetic norms is predicated a new and fluid hierarchy of theatrical elements, whereby temporary ascendancy is enjoyed in turn by director, actor, designer, even spectator. Often, now, the burden of signification, lifted from the playwright and his linguistic text, divides itself more equitably between various theatrical elements and entities, creating not only new techniques and effects, but also new subjects. Of the latter, perhaps the most fertile turns out to be the stage itself, the stage as object of aesthetic experimentation and philosophical contemplation, the so-called "self-conscious" stage of modern drama. (1986: 8)

The phenomenon of self-referring is not uncommon in the twentieth century; in fact, some critics such as Whiteside (1988: 27) maintain that all theatrical signs are self-referential: "a theatrical sign is both a sign and a referent, a hyphenated sign-referent: at once a sign of something and the thing or things referred to by the actors. Thus, the concrete theatrical referent seen onstage refers, in turn, to itself as a mimetic theatrical sign" (it is interesting to note that Peirce says that "every sign . . . signifies primarily that it is a sign" [CP 5.313]. As Rokem (1986: 2) says, the spectator, even in a realistic performance, is always aware that he is not watching real people, and (as Johansen [1986b] maintains) that the space being observed has been set aside specifically for a theatrical performance, separating it from real life. The spectator, in other words, perceives the stage as a stage and not as a reproduction of a place that exists outside the theatrical space (cf. Quigley 1985: 25). However, the spectator can slip into moments in which he does not separate the fiction of the stage—the illusion of reality—from reality.

The question here is when does the spectator get beyond the point of simply recognizing that the performance is theater and think of it in terms of theater and reality (art and life)? I believe this starts or is provoked by self-referring devices that are encoded into the performance, often with the specific intention of provoking such thoughts. These devices are not always immediately obvious in Nelson's dramas because he follows a story line that holds the spectator's attention while at the same time imposing upon him the theatrical nature and being of the work. The works reveal rather than hide their dramatic devices and draw attention to their own composition as fictional constructs. The devices range from the obvious to the subtle—from actors moving or removing stage props to construct or dismount a scene (*Vestido de noiva*), to the use of the chorus (*Álbum de família; Anjo negro*), to the creation of fictional worlds by characters within the fictional construct of the text (*Anjo negro*) itself. The devices are usually closely tied to an overall examination of the human being's reading and misreading of signs that make up his individual and collective universes. The texts thus comment on their own creative processes and foreground relevant issues such as the antinomy between illusion and reality in human existence while paralleling the question of the relationship between art and life. This felicitous interaction and conspiracy of form and content (i.e., theatrical devices and themes) is present in most of Nelson's dramas, but particularly in those written in the 1940s and early 1950s (specifically those Magaldi classifies as psychological and mythic). These works are marked by a timeless universe inhabited by beings that are between mythic and psychological types and flesh and blood creations (e.g., Ismael is a mythic type, but the playwright also provides a few markers that link him to a specific Brazilian setting as he does with Alaide, who is more a psychological case study but also tied at specific moments in the text to the city of Rio de Janeiro). On the level of type—either mythic or psychological—almost totally divorced from external extratextual reality, Nelson can explore basic, essential human nature and values without binding his work temporally to specific political, social, or economic issues. And departing from this level, he can examine theater in its essence, those moments when life and art merge and separate, where the spectator is manipulated between fictive universe of the text and extratextual reality and placed into the humanly ambiguous situation of not always being able to tell clearly one from the other.

The text functions on a number of levels at various moments of its unfolding—i.e., it functions as various signs. It is a total sign in itself, composed, of course, of a complex structure of different types of signs that are transformed and modified over the course of the text as the spectator interprets and moves toward some kind of final understanding. These understandings (or interpretants) do not necessarily appear simultaneously as a finished, neat product which the spectator takes home when the performance is finished and the stage space reverts to its place in the real world as simply that—i.e., a stage space, when it ceases to be a magical space supporting possible worlds. On the contrary, throughout the performance, the spectator, at any one point, has some understanding; however, this may be corrected, eliminated, modified, or amplified as the total context of signs—i.e., characters, events, objects, etc.—on the stage is realized.

In the case of Nelson's plays, the spectator often comes slowly into knowledge of the textual world because of the enigmatic quality that distracts from and makes impossible any facile interpretation. Often the spectator accompanies a character who arrives at the same moment at the same understanding; this character searches through the labyrinth of facts and fantasy for some understanding of his/her personal situation within the fictive world as the spectator attempts to understand the fictive world from the outside. In *Vestido de noiva*, it is Alaide who, at the same time as the spectator, relives her memories and lives out her fantasies as she tries to arrive at an understanding of her life in its final moments; in *Anjo negro*, it is the character Ismael who finally understands that he is what he is—i.e., a black man in a white world—and that he cannot change and must live with this. The spectator, however, goes beyond the characters; the spectator always possesses a privileged position and can go beyond mere details of existence as it is portrayed in the actions and speeches of his fictive counterparts. The spectator can see the work as a reflection of itself, as a sign of itself. The character can only read the signs of the fictive world; he/she can never relate to the world beyond the stage space or the pages of the printed script.

The ever-present questioning of reality and what defines it is never concretely resolved in Nelson's theater; it is left in a somewhat ambiguous and vague area where the spectator, at times, thinks that reality can be separated from illusion and defined. At other times, the spectator sees a more comprehensive reality, one composed of a fluid combination of both the real and the imaginary. The important aspect is that Nelson reveals that steadfast, inflexible definitions and categorizations do not exist, or if they do, they exist only for brief moments, to be replaced by others that are just as ephemeral. This instability of perception may be seen reflected in the metatheatrical qualities of Nelson's texts, and may be seen as a reflection of the instabilities of a world that no longer stands up under a positivistic examination. As Waugh (1984: 7) says of metafictional writing, it is both a response and a contribution to an even more thorough-going sense that reality or history are provisional: no longer a world of eternal verities but a series of constructions, artifices, impermanent structures. The materialist, positivistic and empiricist world-view on which realistic fiction is premised no longer exists.

Through their metatheatrical qualities Nelson's texts are thus signs of themselves and, at the same time, signs of both the social and the artistic aspects of the world in which they were produced.

The plays selected for this study include three of the playwright's first four, and were written in the decade of the 1940s. The first, *A mulher sem pecado* (1941), has been omitted; although it contains elements of what constitutes the underlying themes and techniques of the dramatist's theatrical works (cf. Magaldi 1981a: 9-15), it was, as Magaldi (1962: 202) says, "ainda um ensaio preparatório" [still a preparatory experiment]. It is with *Vestido de noiva* (1943) that Nelson Rodrigues' talents as a playwright truly emerge and his career begins. It is also with this text that Brazilian theater enters the twentieth century. Two types of plays indicated by Magaldi in his recent editions of Nelson's work—the psychological and the mythic plays—are represented in here, as are the major innovations and themes of this phase of the playwright's career. The plays, in addition to constituting part of what is referred to as the first phase of the author's theater, were selected as examples of the specific issues and problems that will serve as the point of departure for the analysis of each in the following chapters. Each chapter constitutes an autonomous study, and may be read as such. However, the examinations of the individual plays gain greater dimensions if seen within the context of the analyses of the various works in this study.

It is my hope that cohesion and unity are achieved through the methods of analysis and the application of these to individual texts of a single playwright within a particular historical context of a national theater. There is necessarily some repetition of theoretical explanations. I believe that the repetitions, rather than references to previous locations in the text, make the task of the reader easier and less chaotic (as does the lack of notes, which generally interrupt the flow of a text; for the convenience of the reader who does not know Portuguese, I have included my own translations in brackets immediately following the original). I also believe that it is more convenient for the reader to have the theoretical notions explained as they are applied (but of course, I am setting myself up as a type of ideal reader). The reader will note that little time or space is devoted to a discussion of biographical details. Such details in themselves would be interesting because Nelson's life in its own way was fascinating; however, these are not necessary for an understanding of his art. His texts have a life of their own and speak for themselves. Nonetheless, I believe that there still emerges from these pages an image of a complex person who is the most important and controversial figure in twentieth-century Brazilian dramaturgy.

CHAPTER II

ICONIC, INDEXICAL, AND SYMBOLIC ASPECTS OF THE SIGN IN *VESTIDO DE NOIVA*

In this chapter I examine Nelson Rodrigues' *Vestido de noiva* (1943) from the point of view that theater is a construct of signs, in both the written and the performance texts, and that the signs manifest themselves iconically, indexically, and symbolically (sometimes a sign functions as all three at the same time—cf. Ransdell 1986: 688) in both texts. The basis of the present study is Peirce's concept of the sign, which consists of the sign in itself (the sign vehicle), the interpretant, and the object:

> A sign, or *representamen*, is something which stands to somebody for something in some respect or capacity. It addresses somebody, that is, creates in the mind of that person an equivalent sign, or perhaps a more developed sign. That sign which it creates I shall call the *interpretant* of the first sign. The sign stands for something, its *object*. (CP 2.228)

Semiosis (communication) occurs when there is total mediation within the triad—i.e., when the interpretant (the sign into which the sign vehicle is translated) mediates between the sign in itself and the object (cf. Buczynska-Garewicz 1982: 8). It is, as Ransdell indicates, "the process whereby reality manifests itself in the understanding." Here Ransdell formulates semiosis in terms of another type of mediation, the sign mediating between object and interpretant: "the object-sign-interpretant relation of semiotic theory is intended to capture the logical form of the the process whereby *reality* (the object) comes into the *mind* (the interpretant) by way of a mediating *phenomenon* (the sign)" (1976: 103). This is the dynamics of sign production in Peircean semiotics: sign produces sign, sign interprets sign (cf. Buczynska-Garewicz [1982: 8], who says that "semiosis may be termed total mediation" and "semiosis is a process of continuous mediation or, as Peirce also writes, of mediating representation." Buczynska-Garewicz also deals with the two types of mediation mentioned above).

Peirce refined and elaborated his definition of the sign over the years with a number of trichotomic divisions. The most exploited of these, particularly by semioticians of theater, is the trichotomy that defines the relation between the sign and its object: the icon, index, and symbol. The icon is a sign vehicle that resembles its object in some way; this similarity may range from the more subtle resemblance of a diagram or a map of a city to the more total reproduction of an object in a realistic painting. The index is causally related to its object in an existential relationship, such as the pointing of a finger to indicate direction or smoke indicating fire. The symbol's relationship to its object is purely conventional and unmotivated; no necessary resemblance or existential relationship exists in this sign function.

The following excerpt from Peirce's writings underscores the relation of the sign vehicle to the object and relates these to the interpretant; it also brings out important points for theater (and literary) semiotics in general—i.e., that fact that the icon's object does not have to exist in fact, and that the symbol would not be a sign without an interpretant:

> A sign is either an *icon*, an *index*, or a *symbol*. An *icon* is a sign which would possess the character which renders it significant, even though its object had no existence; such as a lead-pencil streak as representing a geometrical line. An *index* is a sign which would, at once, lose the character which makes it a sign if its object were removed, but would not lose that character if there were no interpretant. Such, for instance, is a piece of mould with a bullet-hole in it as a sign of a shot; for without the shot there would have been no hole; but there is a hole there, whether anybody has the sense to attribute it to a shot or not. A *symbol* is a sign which would lose the character which renders it a sign if there were no interpretant. Such is an utterance of speech which signifies what it does only by virtue of its being understood to have that signification. (CP 2.304)

Esslin has noted, "Clearly, but also somewhat paradoxically, the specific nature of theater makes it more concerned with icons (images, representations of people and things) and indices (gestures) than with symbols" (1982: 1). Esslin (1987: 43-44) approaches the dramatic performance as a "fictional or otherwise represented reality." It is, in other words, essentially iconic, but all three types of signs necessarily operate within this "basic iconic mimesis."

Elam (1980: 22-27), on the other hand, deals with the iconic, indexical, and symbolic functions of signs on stage and concludes that "theatrical performance as a whole is symbolic, since it is only through convention that the spectator takes stage events as standing for something other than themselves.... It can be said, therefore, that on stage the symbolic, iconic and indexical sign-functions are co-present: all icons and indices in the theatre necessarily have a conventional basis" (Elam 1980: 27). Both critics are correct; they simply approach the issue from two different angles. Deely's (1985: 34) observation that "the development of theater... largely depends on the symbolic dimensions that can be introduced into iconicity itself" completes and puts both approaches into perspective. The important point is that all three types of signs are always present in any performance and the meaning(s) of both written and performance texts will often emerge from the tension created by the foregrounding and backgrounding of the various types. Fisch (1986: 333) discusses the icon, index, and symbol as aspects of semeioses that vary in prominence:

> ... just as the world does not consist of two mutually exclusive kinds of things, signs and non-signs, so there are not three mutually exclusive kinds of signs: icons, indices, and symbols. These are rather elements or aspects of semeioses that vary greatly in relative prominence or importance from semeiosis to semeiosis. We may therefore call a sign, for short, by the name of that element or aspect which is most prominent in it, or to which we wish to direct attention, without thereby implying that it has no element or aspect of the other two kinds.

Kowzan's (1968) classification of theatrical signs into thirteen systems will be used in this analysis. However, I hope to avoid what one critic has found to be a shortcoming of Kowzan's work: "[it] categorized theatrical performance as a series of thirteen separate codes, but failed to tackle the vital problem of their interrelation and simultaneous operation" (Issacharoff 1981: 262). It should also be noted that there are several other shortcomings of the typology. Van Zyl (1979: 100) has pointed out that Kowzan failed to take into consideration the spectator as an important aspect among the various theatrical sign systems. Elam (1980: 50) and Esslin (1987: 53) have noted the lack of mention of the architectural features of the playhouse and the stage. Esslin considers these features to be "framing and preparatory indicators" that prepare the audience for perceiving signs in a specific way—i.e., as theatrical signs. As he says, "It is the stage . . . itself which acts as a primary generator of meaning. However trivial an object or an event may appear in the 'real' world, as soon as it is perceived on a stage . . . it is immediately raised to the level of a sign" (1987: 53; cf. Rozik [1983: 67], who, in describing the language of theater as phenomenological, says, "The structure of the theatre's auditorium and the nature of the theatrical event are the signal for the audience to shift from the code of natural language, and from their accustomed attitude to natural phenomena, to the code of phenomenological language"). The type of stage (e.g., proscenium arch or theater in the round) and location (e.g., in a church or in a cabaret) exercise an important influence on audience expectations and reading of the signs of the performance. Even with these omissions in his work, Kowzan's typology, as Elam (1980: 51) notes, identifies the most important theatrical sign systems, and to date no scholar or critic has offered a more complete or systematic classification.

Therefore, I intend to use Kowzan's classification and Peirce's semiotic theories to show that text production is a dynamic process of sign production, that meaning is generated by a constantly shifting perception of signs created by a constant foregrounding of sign function in Nelson Rodrigues' play: indexical elements in iconic systems, symbolic elements in iconic systems, indexical elements in symbolic systems, with a final expressive symbolic pattern emerging as a result of the tension among the iconic, indexical, and symbolic elements at various moments of the play's action (cf. Pladott 1982: 36-39). It was because of this process, or rather how the manifestation of it was achieved technically on the stage under Ziembinski's direction and with Santa Rosa's set designs, that *Vestido de noiva* represented such an important moment in the evolution of Brazilian theater. And it was through this process that Nelson Rodrigues contributed to the revitalization and regeneration of an automatized, lifeless theater which continued to cling to traditions established in the nineteenth century ("um panorama cenico ainda dominado por comédias de pequeno alcance" [a theatrical panorama still dominated by comedies of little importance]—Magaldi 1981b: 21). In this work, which, because of its technical and thematic innovations, is one of the most important theatrical pieces staged in this century in Brazil, the playwright deforms and exaggerates the existing canons of theater and produces a more abstract, symbolic form of representation. He helps to bring Brazilian theater more within the realm of contemporary esthetics, which is nonmimetic (but not, however, antimimetic, as Hornby indicates):

> The whole tenor of contemporary aesthetics is nonmimetic. This is, again, not the same thing as antimimetic. The mimetic aspect of art is not denied, but it is no longer seen as its defining trait. (Hornby 1986: 16)

At the same time, Nelson Rodrigues captures human nature and existence with a greater degree of accuracy and meaning for his audience than he could have by portraying his vision through a theater dominated by the iconic (mimetic) function.

Lins (1975: 65) speaks of the realism achieved by Nelson as a "realismo total" [total realism], which is an amplification of naturalistic realism achieved through poetic intuition:

> O conhecimento dos fenômenos psíquicos apresentados em *Vestido de noiva* só poderia ser feito de maneira a-lógica e intuitiva. O seu caminho era a intuição poética para atingir o realismo total, que é uma ampliação em profundidade do realismo naturalista: o seu processo era criar uma lógica para as manifestações a-lógicas, uma verossimilhança capaz de acompanhar os movimentos de liberdade da imaginação em delírio.
>
> [Knowledge of the psychic phenomena presented in *Vestido de noiva* could only have been made possible in an a-logical and intuitive manner. The route taken to achieve the total realism, which is an extremely profound amplification of naturalistic realism, was poetic intuition: the process was that of creating a logic for the a-logical manifestations, a verisimilitude capable of accompanying the movements of the freedom of the delirious imagination.]

Jakobson has shown that realism is an ambiguous, arbitrary term determined by conventions and rules, and the perceiver has to know the conventions in order to discern the illusion of reality in the work of art. As Jakobson (1987c: 21) says of painting, the "conventional, traditional aspect . . . to a great extent conditions the very act of our visual perception. As tradition accumulates, the painted image becomes an ideogram, a formula, to which the object portrayed is linked by contiguity. Recognition becomes instantaneous. We no longer see a picture. The ideogram needs to be deformed." The same applies to the theater, and to a great extent it seems that Nelson accomplishes in his text what the Russian painter mentioned in Jakobson's article attempted to accomplish on his canvases–i.e., he intentionally deforms and creates disorder in order to impose new modes of perception on the spectator while attempting to approximate reality more closely (cf. also Jakobson's essays "Futurism" [1987b] and "Dada" [1987a], in which he discusses the notion of realism in art). As he does this in all his theater, Nelson expounds the need for a constant reorganizing of current ideas about reality and art– i.e., the need constantly to change the usual patterns of perception. Along these lines, it is interesting to note that Kuhner [1971: 50-51) maintains that Nelson's theater, like Brazilian theater in general, is realistic:

> Mas uma análise mais minuciosa de suas peças mostrará que, neste caso, como nos demais, a utilização de recursos expressionistas, no plano cênico, não parte da atitude fundamental de negação da realidade objetiva, que iniciou o expressionismo. Pelo contrário, o teatro de Nelson Rodrigues. . . é realista, como todo o nosso teatro, e aqueles recursos servem de fato a uma visão da realidade, a uma crítica social, no caso de Nelson, moralizante, individualista e subjetiva. Insere-se, por estes traços, na linha que atravessa o teatro brasileiro a partir de Martins Pena.
>
> [But a more detailed analysis of his plays will show that, in this case, as in the others, the use of expressionistic devices, on the scenic level, does not depart from the fundamental attitude of the negation of objective reality, which began with Expressionism. On the contrary, Nelson Rodrigues' theater . . . is realistic, like all of our theater, and those devices, in fact, serve to create a vision of reality, a social criticism, in the case of Nelson, a moralizing, individualistic and subjective one. Because of these

traits, it enters into a line that traverses Brazilian theater beginning with Martins Pena.]

The point of departure of this analysis is one particular cluster of signs in the text: the initial auditory ones that introduce the spectator to the work in which the playwright explores and deautomatizes a traditional love triangle of two sisters vying for the same man. In this text the protagonist, Alaide, has been struck by an automobile and spends her final moments reconstructing her past through memory and fantasy. The play for the most part takes place in her mind, and centers on the conflict with her sister Lucia. The lack of order caused by the incessant fragmentation of the self and the search for a center or wholeness are ideas that characterize much of modern art. The search for a restoration or creation of a sense of order is a quest for understanding and meaning. Alaide is a prime example of this; she exists in fragments, torn among external reality, memory, and fantasy, but desperately seeking coherence and unity by probing into the past for those meaningful bits and pieces that will explain her self to herself. In general, Nelson's plays constitute a world peopled by fragmented beings searching for meaning. However, this is a world in which paradox, irony, and ambiguity are the norm, and in each text we see that these essential features *are* the coherence and unity in this world.

The auditory signs, which belong to the sign system of sound effects (according to Kowzan [1968: 72], these are sounds that "being natural or artifical signs in life, are artificially reproduced for aims of the spectacle"), create an immediate sense of violence and disaster. They are repeated, with some slight variations, at crucial moments throughout the text as the story develops. The cluster thus comes to represent a constant in what appears to the spectator to be a chaotic, disjointed plot. The perception of these initial signs (and then their repetition) and the necessity of contextualization and re-perception of them by the spectator represents the matrix process of perception and understanding of the entire text. Although I disagree and believe that he did not understand the significance of the repetition of the sounds of the accident, it is interesting to note that one critic found the repetition of these to be a defect; he believed that the audience could find the repetition humorous:

> Outro pormenor a evitar é a repetição de qualquer passagem. Quero referir-me especialmente às repetições dos discos de ruídos do desastre de automóveis e chegada da ambulância. A freqüência desses truques conduz sempre ao risco do humorismo—e penso que neste ponto até mesmo Bergson ajuda a minha afirmação. Não foi difícil sentir na platéia, na terceira ou quarta audição do disco, os primeiros sintomas dessa reação, certamente não desejada pelo autor . . . (Figueiredo 1975: 111-112)

> [Another detail to avoid is the repetition of any passage. I am referring especially to the repetitions of the recordings of the sounds of the accident and the arrival of the ambulance. The frequency of these devices always leads to the risk of humor—and I think that even Bergson would agree with my affirmation. It was not difficult to sense in the audience, on hearing the recording for the third or fourth time, the first symptoms of this reaction, which the author certainly did not intend].

The first contact between viewer and possible world to be created on the stage occurs with the stage space in total darkness (without the use of a front curtain). The sounds of a car horn, violent skidding, breaking of glass, and an ambulance siren are heard:

> Microfone—Buzina de automóvel. Rumor de derrapagem violenta. Som de vidraças partidas. Silêncio. Assistência. Silêncio. (Rodrigues 1981a: 109; subsequent references to the text are to this edition)

> [Microphone: A car horn. A violent skidding sound. Sound of breaking glass. Silence. Ambulance siren. Silence.] (Rodrigues 1980: 23; subsequent translations of the text are from this edition)

The sounds are, as Lima Lins (1979: 63) says, "a primeira informação que atinge a platéia. Trata-se de um fato exterior explorado e apresentado como tal, por intermédio de ruídos conhecidos . . . A primeira vista, nada de novo. O público está cansado de ter experiências semelhantes quase todos os dias" [the first information that reaches the audience. It is a question of an external fact explored and presented as such, through known sounds . . . At first glance, nothing new. The public is weary from having similar experiences almost daily]. There is established in these few moments, as suggested by the Brazilian critic, an iconic system within the text: the spectator hears the sounds and perceives them as qualities, unreflectedly, of the real thing. And it is important to note here, as Esslin has (1987: 43), that not all iconic signs are visual: "[t]he sound of a car horn in a play is an icon of the sound of a car horn." It is only when the other sign systems (particularly light and verbal discourse) come into play that the viewer is alerted to something different and strange. This is when the voice of a character is heard over a sound system and the light is slowly raised on one level of the stage; the supposed banality of the sounds of the accident is negated, only to be reaffirmed by the end of the play: "[O] espectador avança e invade um novo campo da realidade para então, perplexo, tomar conhecimento de um drama e admitir que o acidente de rua era do mesmo a manifestação mais banal" [the spectator advances and invades a new area of reality then, perplexed, to learn of a drama and admit that the accident in the street was indeed a most banal occurrence] (Lima Lins 1979: 64).

The selection and combination of the signs are such as to create an impact, and thus a reflection; the indexical function emerges almost immediately as the entire cluster becomes one sign pointing to an automobile accident. The moments of silence observed at two points in the syntagm function indexically also, serving as temporal markers indicating time elapsed before and after the arrival of the ambulance. The darkness of the stage participates in this function as well, suggesting time and/or place: night/and or a space other than the stage space, so that the accident is not visualized. At this point the spectator cannot perceive any of the signs beyond their iconic and indexical levels, which, as Pladott (1982: 36) has shown, converge in the theatrical sign, "while iconicity takes indexical elements, such as gesture, costume, etc., for granted." Immediately following this segment, however, the audience, as noted above, is alerted to a threatening of the iconic function as other theatrical sign systems emerge and begin to form a pattern that will characterize the entire text: a stable symbolic pattern in tension with increasingly unstable iconic and indexical elements. The mimetic features of the text, in other words, will be subsumed by a strongly abstract, symbolic element.

One aspect of the performance text for which Nelson has been acclaimed is his use of lighting, which in essence is a technical system and which has become extremely important in the modern theater. The importance of light in the theater in relation to the spectator is emphasized by Simonson:

> Our emotional reaction to light is more rapid than to any other theatrical means of expression, possibly because no other sensory stimulus moves with the speed of light, possibly because, our earliest inherited fear being a fear of the dark, we inherit with it a primitive worship of the sun. The association between light and joy, between sorrow and darkness, is deeply rooted and tinges the imagery of almost every literature and religion. (1979: 40)

Kowzan (1968: 70) includes light as one of his thirteen categories of theatrical sign systems and notes that "with its perfected mechanisms of distribution and command, [it] has an increasingly wide and rich use from the semiological viewpoint, on the indoor stage as well as in open-air spectacle." Among the more important functions of light, according to Kowzan, are its capabilities of defining the theatrical space, isolating characters or objects and pointing up the relation between them and their surroundings on stage, and enhancing or giving new value to signs of other systems (i.e., gesture, decor, movement —cf. Kowzan 1968: 70).

When Nelson Rodrigues encoded the orchestration of light (and darkness) into his text in the early 1940s, he was breaking with the more antiquated techniques of lighting the entire stage space and giving equal emphasis to each part of that space and the characters and decor that inhabited it. Where he drew from in his innovative (for Brazil of the time) explorations of the value of light in relation to other sign systems of theatrical text (or in almost any of the innovations, thematic or technical, in the play) is a mystery, one which the playwright himself never helped to solve. He supposedly had read only one play and had been to the theater only once (as a child) before he wrote *Vestido de noiva*. As Nelson once said:

> De fato, eu, quando escrevi "Vestido de noiva" não ia a Teatro; não lia nada de Teatro e muito menos Oswald de Andrade. Sabia apenas que existia alhures um tal de William Shakespeare. Foi escrevendo a "Mulher sem Pecado" e "Vestido de Noiva" que descobri o Teatro. Ele brotou de dentro de mim, como se jamais tivesse existido. Foi realmente uma experiência fantástica. (Letter to the author from Nelson Rodrigues, dated May 16, 1980)

[In fact, when I wrote "Vestido de noiva" I was not going to the theater; I did not read any theater, and much less Oswald de Andrade. I only knew that there existed elsewhere a certain William Shakespeare. It was while writing "Mulher sem pecado" and "Vestido de noiva" that I discovered Theater. It sprouted within me, as if it had never existed. It was really a fantastic experience.]

The theatrical scene in Brazil at the time offered little that could account for influences on the playwright; except for the experimental, avant-garde texts of Oswald de Andrade (which Nelson says he did not know), the famed Semana da Arte Moderna [Week of Modern Art], which had been responsible for modernization in other genres and arts, had produced nothing in the way of the art of the stage. As Magaldi (1967: 7) has explained, the synthetic nature of theater (i.e., its quality of combining various arts and technical systems) achieved in Oswald's works prevented their being performed because neither the theatrical conditions nor the talent existed at the time in Brazil. This situation persisted until World War II, as Lima Lins (1979: 55) notes, when a number of European directors fled to Brazil and "traziam técnicas de montagem completamente inéditas no Brasil" [brought staging techniques that were completely unprecedented in Brazil].

Nelson Rodrigues, although recognizing a certain debt to the genius and collaboration of the Polish director Ziembinski, has categorically denied that he collaborated on anything other than the staging of the text: "Ziembinski não concorreu com uma vírgula para o texto. Fez maravilhosamente o que lhe competia como diretor, e só" (1977a: 386) [Ziembinski did not contribute even a comma to the text. He did a marvelous job in what he had to do as a director, but that is all he did]. The playwright, obviously suspecting skepticism on the part of critics and theater historians, explained the avant-garde nature of *Vestido de noiva* as a mystery and miracle (perhaps tongue-in-cheek, since Nelson was a master of irony): "Acho que o meu negócio com o teatro é mediúnico. Uma coisa tão extraordinária que se pode pensar em milagre, um mistério total da personalidade" (Rodrigues 1977b: viii-ix) [I believe that my experience in the theater is somewhat unique. An extraordinary thing that can only be thought of in terms of a miracle, a total mystery of the personality]. Whatever the circumstances in Brazil, and whatever Nelson's personal situation at the time, there did exist a tradition of innovation and the vanguard in theater in Europe and North America.

In relation to stage lighting, much of what Nelson achieved in *Vestido de noiva* affirmed (since we are cautious not to say "influenced by") this tradition, which dates back to the Swiss theoretician Adolphe Appia (cf. Simonson [1979: 47], who discusses Appia's legacy to twentieth-century theater and concludes that his influence is indirect, but nonetheless important: "[O]ur experiments amplified Appia's theories almost before we knew his name, had seen his drawings, or had heard a quotation from his published work. Appia's first two volumes contain the germinal ideas that have sprouted, almost without exception, into the theories of modern stagecraft that we listened to"). Notions of Appia that are reflected in Nelson's use of light in *Vestido de noiva* (according to Ziembinski [1975: 56], there were 174 shifts in lighting throughout his staging of the text) include plastic elements, in that the painted backdrop so typical of nineteenth-century theater is replaced by space created by light, thus creating a true sense of tridimensionality; scene painting, in that light is used to evoke emotional values through its constant shifting of the dramatic emphasis from one scene to another, one actor to another, one prop to another, and the shifting from light to dark; the unifying power of light, making actor, prop, and stage space into one; and the defining, revealing, and isolating of characters, props, or space for various effects and creation of meanings. Nelson uses both types of lighting indicated by Appia. Floodlighting (i.e., diffused, even lighting over a large area) is used to allow visibility of objects and characters without creating a particular emotional response in the spectator; spotlighting (i.e., a concentrated light which is mobile) is used to isolate and define, thus creating a response in the viewer as it accents and emphasizes form. Nelson also employs variations on the two: area lighting (only a portion rather than the entire stage is lighted); fade-ins and fade-outs; and varying intensities–halflighting ("luz amortecida em penumbra"), light to suggest moonlight ("luz lunar"). It is interesting to note that, in Nelson's (1977a: 134) description of the situation of stage lighting in Brazil in 1943, he does recognize Ziembinski's importance as an innovator in this aspect of the theater: "Em 1943, o nosso teatro não era iluminado artisticamente. Pendurava-se, no meio do palco, uma lâmpada de sala de visitas ou de jantar. Só. E a luz fixa, imutável–e burríssima–nada tinha a ver com os textos e os sonhos da carne e da alma. Ziembinski era o primeiro, entre nós, a iluminar poética e dramaticamente uma peça" [In 1943 our theater was not lighted artistically. There was a living or dining room type of light hanging in the middle of the stage. And the stationary, unchangeable–and extremely idiotic–light had nothing to do with the texts and the dreams of the flesh and the soul. Ziembinski was the first among us to light a play artistically and dramatically].

Shortly after *Vestido de noiva* opens, the spectator realizes that lighting functions as an index of temporal and spatial shifts–i.e., it is used to create different time periods and locations. These shifts do not follow a logical, linear pattern or sequence of development in terms of external reality, but as the text ends, the audience realizes that they are iconic of the protagonist's (Alaide's) state of mind. Lighting is used for the creation of disparate times and spaces on two physical levels of the stage where the protagonist lives out her fantasies and relives her memories in the final moments of her life. In the written text these areas are designated "Memória"(Memory) and "Alucinação" (Hallucination; a mixture of delirium and fantasy):

(Cenário–dividido em três planos. 1o. plano: alucinação; 2o. plano: memória; 3o. plano: realidade. Quatro arcos no plano da memória; duas escadas laterais. Trevas.) (p. 109)

[Setting–the stage is divided into three levels. The first level represents Hallucination, the second Memory, and the third Reality. There are four archways on the level of Memory, and two lateral stairways. The stage is in darkness as the play opens.] (p. 23)

In the performance text, however, it is only over the course of the play and the interaction of the various sign systems that the significance of each level is revealed. Lighting, then, is foregrounded and assumes the symbolic function of conveying the chaotic mood and state of mind of Alaide and underscoring the tension between the real and the illusory. Scenes are short and fast-paced as the action is shifted from one level to another; lighting is used to effect these changes, emphasizing and de-emphasizing specific places and times as they pass through the mind of the dying woman. Light is usually on the one area where the action is occuring–i.e., a space or area (usually part of one level) is isolated and foregrounded by light from the rest of stage, which remains in darkness.

Nelson also uses spotlights to isolate a particular character or group of characters without lighting the entire level, and in at least one instance he uses this device to isolate and emphasize, then juxtapose two separate groups of characters. In this instance (Act II) light is used as a sign of memory, fantasy, and the contrast of the two; the contrast is taken even further, however, as the contents of the two lighted spaces are associated with a funeral (level of Hallucination where Alaide is fantasizing Madame Clessi's funeral) and wedding (level of Memory where the protagonist is remembering her own wedding). The scene is a well orchestrated play of lights that includes the protagonist, if I interpret Nelson's stage directions correctly, strolling between the two levels—each one lighted to distinguish it from the other (i.e., not floodlighting on the entire stage, but rather area lighting on each of these levels)— accompanied by a spotlight. The light on Alaide (and her movements) is then used to emphasize her role as a sign unifying the chaos on the stage; she is what unifies and gives meaning to the disparate times: the present moment of her memory (which is, of course, a past) and the past of her fantasy. As the two spaces are one—Clessi's house in the past, Alaide's in the present—the two times are really one in that they exist only in the unifying consciousness (or unconsciousness, in this case) of the protagonist. The entire scene consists of interpretants (i.e., signs created as interpretants in the mind of Alaide); what occurs on the stage is the way she sees (remembers and fantasizes) the signs around her. The audience, then, perceives signs that are created specifically as interpretant signs (and these of course become interpretants in the spectator as he perceives and interprets the events on the stage).

There are sporadic intrusions of external circumstances of the moment effected through the use of light. When this occurs, the levels of *Memória* and *Alucinação* are darkened, and the third level, that of *Realidade*, is illuminated. External reality consists of brief moments when the mental levels are suspended and Alaide's mind does not project her memories or fantasies onto the stage; the moments are short scenes in which reporters talk about Alaide's accident, doctors attempt to save her life, and (in Act III, after the protagonist's death) her sister gets married. Total darkness, an important element of lighting in the text, functions both indexically and symbolically. It is indexical of shifts of time and space (from memory to hallucination, from Alaide's mind to external reality), but it also assumes the symbolic function of revealing the protagonist's inability or refusal to remember certain details of her life—particularly the identity of the veiled woman, which plagues Alaide almost to the end of the second act (p. 144) and which is an essential bit of information in her reconstruction of her wedding.

The stage space, according to Nelson's sidetext, is essentially bare, with only the minimum of scenic metonymy to indicate place. The empty space, however, is transformed from the traditional one-level stage into a multilevel conjunct of three different physical spaces (to which the spectator is introduced early in the text) which will represent different temporal spaces. My assumption (and I assume it was Nelson's also) in dealing with stage space—that space set aside and agreed upon by performers and spectators as an area of representation—is that it functions as a sign, or perhaps a multiplicity of signs, that conveys essential information to the viewer. This information may be relayed in a number of ways—there is a semantic content in the stage space itself in that it signals that it is a space where a performance is about to occur; there is then the space between characters, between actor and spectator, between props and characters, and (of particular interest in *Vestido de noiva*) the space between various areas of the stage. The significance of these spaces is determined by spatial codes that are both theatrical and cultural, depending upon the conventions of both—theatrical in the sense of what the stage space will allow in terms of distances, etc., and cultural in the sense of how a given group behaves in terms of physical proximity or distance. Hall's work on proxemics ("the interrelated observations and theories of man's use of space"— 1966: 1) defines these proxemic manifestations: *infracultural* ("behavioral and . . . rooted in man's biological past"), *precultural* ("physiological and very much in the present"), and *microcultural* ("the one on which most proxemic observations are made") (1966: 101). The microcultural, which is subdivided into fixed-feature, semi-fixed feature, and informal, has been incorporated into the study of theatrical subcodes by Elam (1980: 62-69). Elam associates the fixed-feature with permanent features of the performance such as the architectural determination of the stage space (i.e., is it theater in the round, proscenium-arch, etc.), the semi-fixed feature with the moveable aspects of the set, and the informal with the space between human beings (between actor and actor and between actor and spectator) involved in the performance. Although these are interrelated and interdependent within and outside the performance, one often determining and limiting the other, we must isolate each of them for analysis and discussion.

The one of interest to us in this performance text may be defined as semi-fixed feature in that it involves the set, but fixed-feature in that it must convince the spectator that the spaces being defined are indeed fixed. This involves the various levels, and how each level may represent various spaces at different times. Each level is semi-fixed in that it is a set and not a permanent part of the playhouse; each level represents specific locations in particular time periods, and thus must convey to the spectator the image of fixed feature (i.e., a sense of the permanent, such as a house, a bedroom in the house, etc.). This is achieved through indices belonging to various systems of signs. Decor, according to Kowzan (1968: 69-70), has as its primary function the identification of geographical space, social place, and time. Space (and time) in *Vestido de noiva* is identified by a limited number of objects, such as a mirror to indicate a bedroom, and a cross to indicate the church where the wedding is to take place. Kowzan (1968: 70) notes that "A spectacle can do entirely without a decor. Its semiological role in this case is played by gesture and movement (an expedient to which pantomime readily has recourse), by the word, sound effects, costumes, accessories and also by the lighting." This is precisely the case in Nelson's play, where the lack of physical indices of decor is of symbolic value and supports the underlying notion of the conflict between the real and the imagined. Costumes ("the most external and conventional means of defining the human being"–Kowzan 1968: 67) and make-up (cf. Kowzan 1968: 66) are sign systems that also define space and time in the text. The house of prostitution, for example, in the opening scene of the play, where Alaide (in her mind) has gone to find Madame Clessi, is indicated visually by the characters' costumes and make-up (and this is strongly emphasized by the contrast created by Alaide's appearance): "3 mesas, 3 mulheres escandalosamente pintadas, com vestidos berrantes e compridos. Decotes .... Alaíde, uma jovem senhora, vestida com sobriedade e bom gosto, aparece na cena. Vestido cinzento e uma bolsa vermelha" (p. 109) [Three tables, three women garishly made up, in gaudy, long dresses. Low necklines .... Alaide, a young woman dressed discreetly and in good taste, appears in the center of the set. Gray dress and a red purse] (p. 23).

The symbolic function of the total stage rapidly becomes apparent, but as I have said, the specific significance of two levels representing mental layers of the protagonist's mind (i.e., they constitute an iconic representation of Alaide's mental processes in her final moments of life) and one signifying external present time is only revealed as the action progresses and the other codes of the text converge into meaningful units. This occurs as the spectator perceives the proxemic code of informal space, the relation of closeness and distance between actors, which is in part determined by the divided stage. Certain characters can appear only on certain levels, and then only at particular moments. Madame Clessi, for example, a prostitute who died before Alaide was born, cannot appear on Reality, and she can be seen on Memory only when Alaide's state of mind disintegrates to the point of confusing fantasy and memory (she is seen in Act III on the level of Memory with her young lover and then in a confrontation with the lover's mother [pp. 136, 155-157]). Madame Clessi, then, is totally a creation of Alaide's mind; she serves a dual function. She represents an escape from the frustrations and boredom of daily existence because she is the antithesis of bourgeois conventions (cf. Lima Lins 1979: 67: "Até lá chegava Alaíde. No conflito com suas frustrações, saía perdendo a formação burguesa, pelo menos no plano da fantasia") [Alaide reached that point. In the conflict with her frustrations, she came out losing her bourgeois formation, at least on the level of fantasy]. She also serves as a pyschiatrist figure, pushing Alaide into reconstructing her memories and separating these from her fantasies. However, since she is a creation of Alaide's mind, it is essentially Alaide pushing herself to remember via Madame Clessi. Newspaper reporters, doctors, etc., who are a part of present external reality, cannot appear on Memory and Hallucination.

While Reality is clearly separated from the mental levels, the latter two are not always so distinctly separated from each other (except in a physical, visual sense in the performance). As Magaldi (1981a: 17) notes

> A distinção dos planos da memória e da alucinação não obedece a fronteiras rígidas. A memória deveria conter-se nos acontecimentos do passado, enquanto as cenas em que aparece Clessi,

por exemplo, perteneceriam naturalmente ao território do delírio. Mas, na mente em decomposição de Alaíde, os dois planos às vezes se confundem e estão inscritos na lembrança episódios que só podem ter consistência no plano alucinatório.

[The distinction between the levels of memory and hallucination does not obey any rigid boundaries. Memory should restrict itself to events from the past, while the scenes in which Clessi appears would naturally belong to the terrritory of delirium. But, in the disintegrating mind of Alaide, the two levels sometimes are confused and there are episodes inscribed in memory that can only be consistent on the hallucinatory level.]

The same actor, for example, is used to play the roles of different characters on each level (the actor playing Pedro also plays the parts of the janitor, the client in the house of prostitution, and Madame Clessi's young lover), and at one point in the text, the protagonist's mind becomes so chaotic that she cannot separate factual memory from fantasy. This is visualized on stage, as I have already noted, by the actress going from one level to the other accompanied by a spotlight. At the same time, both areas are lighted, and contrasting scenes are constructed around a funeral on the level of Hallucination (Clessi's funeral some forty years earlier) and a wedding on that of Memory (Alaide's, only a few years earlier). Different time periods and occasions for the two spaces are created indexically through costume: the characters on Hallucination are dressed to suggest the early 1900s (for Clessi's funeral) while those on Memory are in costumes that indicate the present moment of the action (the 1940s). The indexicality of this sign system does not threaten the already well-established symbolic systems of lighting and decor; on the contrary, the tension of indexical and symbolic elements generates the contrasts of memory/fantasy, past/present, and real/unreal which by the end of the play are accommodated into a meaningful unit for the spectator.

The positioning of the areas of the stage functions within the symbolic mode also; the spectator may read this as a mental hierarchy in relation to Alaide's state of mind: Reality, in which Alaide does not intrude, is farthest from the audience; Memory, which is a mixture of accurate and faulty remembrances, occupies a medial position (i.e., it is somewhere between the real and unreal); Hallucination, which often predominates over both memory and external reality, is the closest to the spectator. Nelson, in other words, has reversed the usual perception of the human being's proximity to reality and fantasy. What emerges is, as Lima Lins (1979: 63) says, the following suggestion: "no campo da nossa consciência, quantos planos percorre a realidade antes que se forme uma conclusão perceptível? Que caminhos, que roteiros sinuosos dão passagem às mensagens vindas de 'fora', para que estas se apresentem a nossa compreensão com a plenitude de seus sentidos" [in the area of the conscious, how many levels does reality traverse before a perceptible conclusion is formed? What paths, what sinuous routes give passage to the messages coming from outside so that these can present themselves to our comprehension in the completeness of their meanings].

Action, played out in the rapid, short scenes effected through the use of lighting, becomes symbolic when the spectator realizes that there is no precise or immediate cause and effect pattern established between the events and incidents. The constant shifts from one level to another, voices heard over a sound system while the entire stage is in darkness, and the repetition of scenes with different characters create an unreal, often absurd atmosphere of play between the logical and the illogical. Iconicity and indexicality can only be established in the motivation of characters and action as the play nears completion and the spectator is able to fit the pieces of Alaide's memories together, sort from this her fantasies, and then accommodate these with the action that occurs on the level of Reality. Even at this point the symbolic still threatens; after Alaide dies in Act III (p. 160) and the levels of Memory and Hallucination are no longer visible, Alaide's voice is still heard over the sound system (pp. 162-163, 164, 166)—she continues to live in Lucia's mind. The level of Reality is also threatened by the mental levels in the final scene. Alaide's death is confirmed by the fact that at one extreme of the level of Reality the spectator sees her tomb. At the other extreme, Lucia is preparing for her wedding to Pedro and asks for her bouquet. Alaide, however, is located on one of the lateral staircases and moves toward Lucia as if to deliver the bridal bouquet. However, before she reaches her sister—i.e., before the unreal can invade the level of Reality—all the characters on stage freeze in position, the stage is darkened, and the text ends:

(*Crescendo de música, funeral e festiva. Quando Lúcia pede o "bouquet", Alaíde, como um fantasma, avança em direção da irmã, por uma das escadas laterais, numa atitude de quem vai entregar o "bouquet". Clessi sobe a outra escada. Uma luz vertical acompanha Alaíde e Clessi. Todos imóveis em pleno gesto. Apaga-se então, toda a cena, só ficando iluminado, sob uma luz lunar, o túmulo de Alaíde. Crescendo da Marcha Fúnebre. Trevas.*) (p. 167)

[Crescendo of the music, the sad and the festive. When Lucia asks for the bouquet, Alaide, like a ghost, advances toward her sister, on one of the lateral stairways, in a manner of someone who is going to deliver the bouquet. Clessi comes up the other stairway. A vertical light accompanies Alaide and Clessi. They stop frozen in their places. The whole set is then darkened, with only the grave of Alaide illuminated as if by moonlight. Crescendo of the Funeral March. Darkness.] (p. 79)

The kinesic code of movements, gestures, facial expressions, etc. functions for the most part iconically and indexically against the background of disconnected, fragmented action. However, at particular moments within this system of theatrical sign (which, because of its predominantly indexical and iconic character, is foregrounded against the symbolic functions of lighting, stage space, and action), a new tension emerges as indexicality is momentarily dominated by symbolic functions. This occurs when actors unexpectedly remove stage props ("Duas mulheres levam 2 cadeiras"–p. 114 [Each of the two women carries a chair off–p. 28]; "O homem carrega a cadeira"–p. 119 [The man carries the chair out–p. 32]) and characters move naturally from one level to the other, violating temporal and spatial barriers. An example of this is the scene in which Alaide, in hopes of finding out what is happening to her, remembers her wedding for the first time. She has just fantasized killing Pedro in previous scenes on the level of Hallucination. As she begins to remember, she moves from Hallucination to Memory with no darkening of the stage; Pedro, at the same time, gets up from the floor and goes to take part in the memory (the playwright stresses that this is to be done in a natural manner: "levantando-se naturalmente e passando também ao plano da memória"–p. 126 [getting up naturally and going also to the level of Memory–p. 39]). The stage is lighted throughout this occurrence and the spectator observes the movement. The symbolic function is accentuated also in the kinesic code in the following instances:

1) *Simultaneous movements of characters*

>Dois homens aparecem no alto das escadas, cada um empunhando dois círios; descem lentamente. (p. 134)

>[Two men appear at the top of the stairs, each one holding two large candles; they descend slowly.] (p. 48)

>Fazem o sinal da cruz, com absoluta coincidência de movimentos. (p. 135)

>[They make the sign of the cross, in a complete coordination of movements.] (p. 48)

>Alaíde, como um fantasma, avança em direção da irmã, por uma das escadas laterais, numa atitude de quem vai entregar o *bouquet*. Clessi sobe a outra escada. Uma luz vertical acompanha Alaíde e Clessi. (p. 167)

>[Alaide, like a ghost, advances toward her sister, on one of the lateral stairways, in a manner of someone who is going to deliver the bouquet. Clessi comes up the other stairway. A vertical light accompanies Alaide and Clessi.] (p. 79)

2) *Pantomime necessitated by the use of invisible props and characters*

>Faz toda a mímica de quem escolhe um disco, que ninguém vê, coloca-o na vitrola também invisível. (p. 110)

>[She does an entire pantomime of someone selecting a record, which no one sees, and placing it on the record player which is also invisible.] (p. 24)

>Rápida e diabólica, Alaíde apanha um ferro invisível, ou coisa que valha, e, possessa, entra a dar golpes. (p. 122)

>[Rapidly and diabolically, Alaide picks up an invisible iron rod, or something similar, and, possessed, she begins to hit him.] (p. 36)

>Cada um puxa pelo braço de um invisível cadáver, arrastando-o. Realizam o respectivo esforço. Arquejam. (p. 123)

>[Each pulls an arm of an invisible corpse, dragging it. Each strains. They gasp.] (p. 37)

Faz um gesto como que apanhando a cauda do invisível vestido de noiva. Faz que se ajeita. (p. 126)

[She makes a gesture, as if picking up the train of the invisible bridal gown. She pretends to adjust the dress.] (p. 39)

Dirige-se a essa pessoa invisível, beijando-a, presumivelmente, na testa. (p. 127)

[She turns toward the invisible person, kissing her, presumably on the forehead.] (p. 40)

3) *Slow motion movements*

Pedro cai em câmara lenta. (p. 122)

[Pedro falls in slow motion.] (p. 36)

4) *Characters walking backwards*

A mãe volta em marcha-à-ré. (p. 126)

[The mother leaves, walking backwards.] (p. 39)

5) *Innumerable times when characters freeze in static positions while sounds are heard from offstage*

Most of these examples occur in Act I, where Alaide's memory is extremely faulty and sketchy. The spectator at these moments is forced to construct a new system in which to understand the changes of sign functions; over the course of the play, he comes to associate them with the other tensions created, and ultimately makes a correspondence between these and Alaide's chaotic, often faulty memory mixed with her fantasies in contrast to the events that occur on the level of Reality. What is foregrounded finally is the play between the real and the imagined within the text.

The verbal code of the text, as the critics have so often noted, is composed of a natural, colloquial language (cf. Barrettini [1980: 159-170]); it is thus iconic, and indexical of a particular region (Rio de Janeiro) and social class (middle class; cf. Lima Lins [1979: 73]:

"Nesta peça, a linguagem é perfeitamente aceitável do ponto de vista de uma moral burguesa"). There is no distortion of syntax or lexical items, but there is at times a foregrounding of the symbolic function within the dialogue. One obvious example of this involves noticeable repetition of segments of dialogue, by Alaide and then by her sister Lucia. At the end of Act I Alaide attempts to reconstruct her wedding, but she is unable at this point to remember all the details. Much of the scene is played out with invisible props and pantomime to indicate the lack of these details. Dona Laura, Alaide's future mother-in-law, enters and addresses an invisible person:

> D. LAURA: Desculpe. Eu não tinha visto você.
>
> (*Pausa para uma resposta que ninguém ouve.*)
>
> D. LAURA (*risonha*):   Quando é o seu?
>
> (*Pausa para outra resposta.*)
>
> D. LAURA (*maliciosa*):   Qual o quê? Está aí, não acredito! Tão moça, tao cheia de vida.
> PAI (*para Alaíde, que está pronta*):   Então vamos!
>
> (*D. Laura faz um gesto qualquer para a invisível pessoa e vai para junto de Alaíde.*)
>
> D. LAURA: Cuidado com a cauda!
>
> (*D. Laura apanha a imaginária cauda e entrega-a a Alaíde.*)
>
> ALAÍDE (*num último olhar*):   Não falta mais nada?
> MAE (*olhando também*):   Nada. Acho que não.
> PAI (*impaciente*):   Já é tarde. Vamos descer.
>
> (*Marcha nupcial. Trevas.*) (pp. 127-128)
>
> [D. LAURA: Excuse me. I didn't see you.
>
> (*She pauses for an answer which no one hears.*)
>
> D. LAURA (*smiling*):   When is yours going to be?
>
> (*She pauses for another answer.*)
>
> D. LAURA (*mischievous*):   No? Come on. I don't believe that! So young. So full of life.
> FATHER (*to Alaide who is ready*):   Well, let's go.

(Dona Laura makes a gesture to the invisible person and goes to stand next to Alaide.)

DONA LAURA: Careful with the wedding train!

(Dona Laura picks up the imaginary train and hands it to Alaide.)

ALAIDE *(with a last look)*: Nothing's missing?
MOTHER *(also looking)*: Nothing. I don't think so.
FATHER *(impatiently)*: It's already late. Let's go down.

(Wedding March. Darkness)] (pp. 40-41)]

In Act II Alaide reconstructs her wedding again, this time with the missing details supplied—specifically the identity of the "invisible woman," the woman in the veil, later to be identified as Lucia. Dona Laura's dialogue is essentially the same; the only difference between this scene and the previous one is the fact that the replies of the "invisible woman" are now heard because she is present in Alaide's memory and can be visualized on stage:

D. LAURA *(para a mulher de véu, que está um pouco retirada)*: Desculpe. Eu não tinha visto você.
MULHER DE VÉU: Não faz mal.

(D. Laura beija-a na testa.)

D. LAURA *(risonha)*: Quando é o seu?
MULHER DE VÉU: Tem tempo! *(noutro tom)* *(com certa amargura)* Nunca!
D. LAURA *(maliciosa)*: Qual o quê! Está aí, não acredito! Tão moça, tão cheia de vida!
PAI *(para Alaíde, que está pronta)*: Então, vamos.

(Som da Marcha Nupcial. D. Laura faz um gesto qualquer para a mulher de véu e vai para junto de Alaíde.)

D. LAURA *(solícita)*: Cuidado com a cauda! *(Apanha a cauda, que entrega a Alaíde)*
ALAÍDE *(num último olhar)*: Não falta mais nada?

(Todos olham, estando situados como no final do 1.º ato)

MAE *(olhando em torno)*: Não. Acho que não.
PAI *(impaciente)*: Já é tarde! Vamos descer!

(Ao som da Marcha Nupcial . . .) (pp. 141-142)

[DONA LAURA *(to the veiled woman who has drawn back):* Excuse me. I didn't see you.
VEILED WOMAN: That's O. K.

(Dona Laura kisses her on the forehead, then smiles)

DONA LAURA: When's yours going to be?
VEILED WOMAN: There's time yet! *(in a different tone, with a certain bitterness)* Never!
DONA LAURA *(mischievous):* What's that! Come on, I don't believe that. So young, so full of life!
FATHER *(to Alaide who is ready):* Well, let's go.

(The sound of the Wedding March. Dona Laura makes a gesture to the woman in the veil and goes to stand next to Alaide.)

DONA LAURA *(solicitously):* Careful with the train! (She picks up the train and hands it to Alaide.)
ALAIDE *(with a last look):* Nothing's missing? *(all look around, being situated as they were in the end of Act I.)*
MOTHER *(looking around):* Nothing. I don't think so.
FATHER *(impatient):* It's already late! Let's go down!

(To the sound of the Wedding March. . .) (pp. 54-55)]

In Act III, after Alaide's death, Lucia is preparing to marry Alaide's husband Pedro. She repeats to Dona Laura almost the same words that Alaide had spoken with the mother-in-law in Act I:

ALAÍDE *(faceira, expondo-se):* Que tal a sua nora? Muito feia?
D. LAURA: Linda. Um amor! (p. 127)

LÚCIA *(com dengue):* Estou muito feia, D. Laura?
D. LAURA: Linda. Um amor! (p. 167)

[ALAIDE *(putting on airs and joking):* How does your daughter-in-law look? Ugly?
DONA LAURA: Beautiful. A dear!] (p. 40)

LUCIA *(with affection):* Do I look very ugly, Dona Laura?
DONA LAURA: Beautiful. A dear!] (p. 79)

The verbal code is foregrounded and becomes symbolic of Alaide's confusion of the real and the unreal in those moments when the stage is darkened and only the voices of either Alaide or Clessi are heard over the sound system, or in those moments when Clessi's voice addresses Alaide. The first instance occurs when Alaide cannot remember enough to visualize on the stage—e.g., in the beginning of Act II the voices of Alaide and Clessi are heard in the darkness with Alaide saying, "Mas não me lembro, Clessi. Estou com a memória tão ruim!..." (p. 129) [But I don't remember, Clessi. My memory is so bad!...–p. 43]; the second when Alaide falters and Clessi urges her along in her memories—e.g., in Act II Alaide has a confrontation with the woman in the veil, Clessi's voice is heard: "Também você não se lembra de nada! Procure vê-la sem véu. Ela não pode ser uma mulher sem rosto. Tem que haver um rosto debaixo do véu" (p. 134) [You still don't remember anything. Try to picture her without the veil. She can't be a faceless woman. There has to be a face under the veil–p. 48].

Other examples of the foregrounding of the symbolic function of the verbal code include characters speaking at the same time ("Os quatro jornaleiros repetem, ao mesmo tempo, os pregões acima" –p. 124 [The four newsboys repeat the above at the same time– p. 38]), and when caricatural gestures demand a corresponding intonation (e.g., the scene in which the confrontation between Madame Clessi and her young lover's mother takes place and there is the parody of *Gone with the Wind*: "Mãe (num largo gesto, visivelmente caricatural, trêmulo na voz)–p. 155 [Mother (in a broad gesture, visibly caricatural, trembling voice)–p. 67]; "Clessi e mãe do namorado. Tom diferente de representação, mas ainda caricatural"– p. 155 [Clessi and the boyfriend's mother. A different tone, but still caricatural–p.68]). Language, however, remains essentially iconic, as does the kinesic code; when it is distorted, the symbolic function captures the spectator's attention and there emerges a tension between the symbolic and iconic-indexical modes of sign production in this subcode of theatrical sign. The entire process of perception then becomes foregrounded and demands a rethinking on the part of the spectator.

One other sign system worthy of note here because of its role in combining with the others to underscore and heighten the constant tension between sign functions is music. Music, as a sign added to the spectacle (as opposed to musical forms of theater such as opera and ballet), functions "to underline, amplify, develop, sometimes belie or replace the signs of the other systems" (Kowzan 1968: 71). Nelson specifies in his text the iconic reproduction of the funeral and wedding marches. The indexical features of these are essentially maintained, indicating Alaide's wedding in Act I (p. 128) and Act II (pp. 141, 147) and her death in Act II (p. 160). The symbolic function, however, emerges when the two pieces are juxtaposed in the final scene capturing the ironic dimensions created here with the contrast of life and death and wedding and funeral—i.e., the confusion and fusion of opposites. Various interpretants emerge as the spectator hears only the Funeral March and the performance ends in darkness. This signals the end of the performance and can be seen as a metacommentary—i.e., the end of the illusion created on the stage. It can also be read as a commentary that compares reality within and outside the theater—i.e., as the end of the performance signifies the end of the fiction created on stage, death, as the ultimate and most definable certainty of reality, signifies the end of life, which has as essential components illusion and dreams.

The initial cluster of auditory signs in the play is repeated five times throughout the text, interspersed among the various sign systems (twice in Act I, once in Act II, twice in Act III):

Buzina. Rumor de derrapagem. Ambulância. Alaíde e Clessi imóveis. (p. 119)

[Horn. Skidding sound. Ambulance siren. Alaide and Clessi frozen.] (p. 32)

Imobilizam-se, emudecem os personagens. Rumor de derrapagem; grito. Ambulância. (p. 124)

[The characters freeze and fall silent. Skidding sound; a shout. Ambulance siren.] (p. 37)

Som de derrapagem. Um grito de mulher. Ambulância. Personagens imóveis. (p. 146)

[Skidding sound. A woman's scream. Siren. Characters frozen.] (p. 59)

Trevas. Disco de derrapagem, grito, ambulância. (p. 151)

[Darkness. Record of the skidding sound, shout, siren.] (p. 64)

Trevas. Luz no plano da alucinação. Estão Alaíde e Clessi imóveis. Rumor de derrapagem. Grito de mulher. Ambulância. (p. 158)

[Darkness. Light on the level of Hallucination. Alaide and Clessi are there frozen. Skidding sound. Woman's scream. Siren.] (p. 70)

After the first use, and the establishment of the iconic and indexical features, however, the playwright varies the combinations of sounds: he repeats the car horn once and then uses only the skidding sound and the ambulance to recreate metonymically the entire sign; there is the addition of the paralinguistic feature of a woman's shout in the third and subsequent instances. The shout attaches a person to the accident, changing the sign value from accident to accident involving a person (who, at the end of Act II, is identified as the protagonist). At this point the spectator can begin to understand Alaide's state of mind, and the levels of the stage begin to come into some kind of perspective and acquire more meaning. The variation of the group of sounds does not threaten the indexicality of the signs; the contexts, however, in which the sounds are used do this, as they foreground the indexicality in relation to the other sign systems. Each time the sounds are heard, the characters freeze into static positions, and the verbal component is momentarily suspended; the action is then resumed, with the characters moving and speaking naturally, as if there had been no interruption. The spectator, because of the other codes in constant interplay, realizes that the characters on the level of Hallucination (and sometimes on the level of Memory) are both living and dead, and that the sounds have as referent the same accident. This destroys the notion that there are a number of different accidents; the spectator thus has to renegotiate these signs into a symbolic function and associate them with Alaide's state of mind—her refusal or inability to remember or fantasize certain details of her life. When she cannot or will not remember, she allows this intrusion of exterior reality to take place and halt the flow of the action. Through contextualization, then, the mimetic, realistic sounds lose their indexical function (i.e., the indexical function is subordinated for purposes of understanding how the sounds of the same accident are heard at different moments as the action progresses), and the spectator comes to view and accept them as he does the other subsystems of the text: symbolic but in constant tension with the iconic and the indexical.

Vestido de noiva represents a break with the theater of its time in that Nelson Rodrigues did not attempt to produce mimetic illusion, the minimal coding of theatrical signs, the foregrounding of subject matter to which the Brazilian public was accustomed. On the contrary, his text foregrounds the esthetic function, drawing attention to the creative process itself. To do this, however, he creates realistic (iconic and indexical) elements and foregrounds these within a predominantly symbolic framework. A tension is thus created with the foregrounding of opposing sign functions, a process which forces the spectator to seek the relation between the sign and the thing signified because of the constantly changing relation between object and sign that is created by context. In terms of what he created at his particular moment in the history of Brazilian theater, he is radical and innovative. As has been said of Beckett, Nelson "actually is placing traditional characters in plots and situations that parody those of traditional drama" (cf. Hornby 1986: 24). However, he achieves this in a most subtle manner, in which the play really speaks about itself and other plays of the period. His text is self-conscious, constantly reminding the spectator that it is theater, that what is occuring on the stage is a performance. The process itself is the meaning generated by the text, which, while contrasting the real and the imagined within, posits the question of art and life to the spectator.

Alaide and the spectator are merged into a similar receiver: both are torn between the mental levels and that of external reality, both confuse memory and fantasy, both attempt to create an order for understanding the shifting sign functions. As Alaide rethinks signs, so the spectator renegotiates the subsystems of theatrical signs. In both the protagonist and the spectator, perception is a dynamic interplay of iconic, indexical, and symbolic functions of signs. Nelson Rodrigues thus creates in his protagonist the process created in the spectator, with the ultimate question emerging in both: what is reality? The answer is the same in both cases: reality is or begins with individual perception and is composed of both what is and what seems; it is a constant interplay of the relation between internal and external, real and imagined, memory and fantasy, life and theater; it is the shifting of the relation between sign vehicle and object.

The great difference between Alaide and the spectator is that the spectator is in a privileged position in relation to the text: he comes to know a reality that Alaide can never know— i.e., his own reality and that of the fictive world of the stage. When the performance ends the spectator can leave Alaide's world, but she can never abandon the fictive constructs of that world. She is always a prisoner of the text and its reality; she is a fictive creation that does not exist beyond the text. The spectator, however, is also a prisoner of his own reality, which he can never abandon completely for the reality of the text.

CHAPTER III

THE PHOTOGRAPHIC IMAGE AND THEATER: MISINTERPRETATION AND INTERPRETATION IN *ÁLBUM DE FAMÍLIA*

Álbum de família was written in 1945, but because of the restrictions of Brazilian censorship, it was not performed until 1967. The text belongs to what Nelson (1949) called his "teatro desagradável" [unpleasant theater], a group of plays intentionally written to provoke strong sentiments and reactions in the spectator. In his *O reacionário*, Nelson explains that after *Vestido de noiva* was a success, he went to the theater and saw a play that was also a total success. It was a piece of light comedy that provoked much laughter. In the third act, however, he suddenly perceived, as he says, a certain truth–that "teatro para rir, com esta destinação específica, é tão absurdo e, mais, tão obsceno como seria uma missa cômica" [theater to provoke laughter, with this specific end, is so absurd and, even more, obscene as would be a comic mass] (1977a: 147). The playwright reveals that from that moment on he had a specific mission as a playwright: to write "teatro desagradável" as opposed to what he had just seen on the stage–i.e., a pleasant, laugh-provoking piece that in no way involved the spectator in the text. He defines "teatro desagradável" and its goals in terms of Brecht's notion of distance. However, in his mind, the distance he wanted to achieve in his texts differed somewhat from the Brechtian distance. Nelson wanted a fusion of spectator and character during the performance; the spectator would forget that he was a spectator and become a man in the fictive world of the stage. However, when the performance was over, the spectator would assume his role in the extratextual world and be able to meditate on love and death.

Nelson's notion concerning distance parallels what he achieves in most of the texts under study in this work—i.e., he confuses reality and illusion and life and theater up to a certain point, and then separates these again allowing for more critical and objective meditation:

> Saí . . . com todo um novo projeto dramático (digo "novo" para mim). O que teria eu de fazer, até o fim da vida, era o "teatro desagradável". Brecht inventou a "distância crítica" entre o espectador e a peça. Era uma maneira de isolar a emoção. Não me parece que tenha sido bem sucedido em tal experiência. O que se verifica, inversamente, é que ele faz toda sorte de concessões ao patético. Ao passo que eu, na minha infinita modéstia, queria anular qualquer distância. A platéia sofreria tanto quanto o personagem e como se fosse também personagem. A partir do momento em que a platéia deixa de existir como platéia—está realizado o mistério teatral.
>
> O "teatro desagradável" ofende e humilha e com o sofrimento está criada a relação mágica. Não há distância. O espectador subiu ao palco e não tem a noção da própria identidade. Está ali como o homem. E, depois, quando acaba tudo, e só então, é que se faz a "distância crítica." A grande vida da boa peça só começa quando baixa o pano. É o momento de fazer nossa meditação sobre o amor e a morte. (Rodrigues 1977a: 147-148)
>
> [I came out . . . with an entirely new dramatic project (I say "new", for myself). What I had to do, until the end of my life, was "unpleasant theater". Brecht invented the "critical distance" between the spectator and the play. It was a way of isolating emotion. It seems to me that he has not succeeded in that experimentation. What happens, on the contrary, is that he makes all sorts of concessions to pathos. While I, in my infinite modesty, wanted to annul any distance that existed. The spectator would suffer as much as the character and as if he were also a character. From that moment in which the audience ceases to be audience—there is realized the theatrical mystery.
>
> "Unpleasant theater" offends and humiliates, and with the suffering the magical relationship is created. There is no distance. The spectator has ascended the stage and has no notion of his own identity. He is there as a man. And, then, when everything is over, and only then, can this critical distance be created. The great life of the good play only begins when the curtain goes down. It is the moment for our meditating on love and death.]

Although *Álbum de família* delves into the collective unconscious of the human mind (cf. Clark and García 1978: 69-78) and focuses on themes of love, hate, incest, suicide, and murder, its basic underlying structure is the same as that which was clearly established in Nelson's important *Vestido de noiva* (1943). This structure is composed of what the critics have referred to as the constant interplay and clash between reality and illusion in human existence. It is, in other words, a foregrounding of human perception of reality. Indeed, Nelson's early plays—in particular those labeled the "comédias míticas" (cf. Pelegrino 1966: 9)—may be characterized as focusing on this as a major theme. In itself, however, this would not be sufficient to guarantee the dramatist his position of importance in Brazilian dramaturgy, since the questioning of the confusion of reality and illusion is as old as literature itself. Nelson's originality and innovation lie in the manner in which he contextualized, on a number of levels of the text (particularly the social and mythical in *Álbum de família*) and at a specific time in the history of Brazilian theater, his concern with man's ability to read and misread signs. It was especially the way in which the playwright indicated the transformation of this into a performance text that attracted the attention not only of audiences but also of directors and other playwrights. Thus, the first staging of *Vestido de noiva* in 1943 (under Ziembinski's direction and with Santa Rosa's set designs) contributed to the transformation of Brazilian theater into a twentieth-century art form, free of the constraints imposed by the persistent and dominating nineteenth-century dramatic and theatrical forms ("comédia de costumes", musical reviews, operettas, historical dramas, etc.), which were incapable of capturing the complexities of twentieth-century man's realities.

In any but the most ideal analyses there are restrictions that inhibit a discussion encompassing all the details of the possible readings of a text, so here I have chosen what I consider to be the crux of the drama—the playwright's concern with the complex association of reality and illusion and the question of realism and truth in art as expressed through the use of the notion of the photographic image—around which other readings, it seems, would have to be structured. The discussion is necessarily based on the written text, but with an imaginary (perhaps ideal) performance in mind. In *Álbum de família*, such an analysis is facilitated by the fact that the author's staging directions are extraordinarily complete and precise;

a director would have to follow these closely or risk transforming the text into an adaptation rather than an accurate representation (cf. Chaudhuri's [1986: 32-33] discussion of performance and adaptation and her proposal for a "semiotics of the performance options of individual texts"). I use the semiotic theory of the American logician Charles S. Peirce as a point of departure for the analysis.

The Peircean concept of sign is of a triadic nature, consisting of the sign in itself (the sign vehicle), the object, and the interpretant:

> A sign, or *representamen*, is something which stands to somebody for something in some respect or capacity. It addresses somebody, that is, creates in the mind of that person an equivalent sign, or perhaps a more developed sign. That sign which it creates I shall call the *interpretant* of the first sign. The sign stands for something, its *object*. (CP 2.228)

This definition becomes more complicated as Peirce elaborates his basic trichotomies of signs, the most fundamental one being the trichotomy that defines the relation between the sign in itself and the object: the division into icon, index, and symbol (CP 2.275). In using Peirce's semiotic, specifically that aspect of relation of sign to object, I believe, as Pladott (1982: 31) has indicated, that it is possible "to avoid such unnecessary antinomies as written text/performance; illusionistic/nonillusionistic theatre"—i.e., questions that have been the focus of much recent theoretical work in semiotics of theater.

The iconic sign is grounded on the principle of similitude; the sign vehicle and the object share a common property which is foregrounded enough to distract from any differences. The similarity may range from a seemingly total reproduction (such as a portrait of a person) to a more subtle resemblance (such as a map of a city). "The iconic function encourages therefore the illusion that reality is truly incarnated on the stage" (Pladott 1982: 31). The indexical sign is grounded on an existential relationship between sign vehicle and object; the connection is causal and may be physical or based on contiguity. The symbol's grounding depends neither on similarity nor on existential relation; the relationship between sign vehicle and object here is unmotivated, therefore conventional. As Pladott notes, in the theater "the symbolic function foregrounds the aesthetic utterance. . . . The arbitrary and conventional relation of the sign to the thing signified . . . minimizes the mimetic illusion, and encourages the spectator to examine the elements of the artistic structure in their own right" (1982: 31).

Based on these definitions, it would seem at first glance that the photograph is an iconic sign. Peirce, however, classifies it as an indexical sign while recognizing the important element of similarity:

> Photographs, especially instantaneous photographs, are very instructive, because we know that they are in certain respects exactly like the objects they represent. But this resemblance is due to the photographs having been produced under such circumstances that they were physically forced to correspond point by point to nature. In that aspect, then, they belong to the second class of signs, those by physical connection. (CP 2.281)

The photograph is indeed an imprint or a trace created by its object—a "freezing mirror", as Eco (1984: 222-223) calls it. However, I agree with Sebeok (1979: 285-286), who believes that Peirce's classification should be read with emphasis on the phrase "in that aspect". In other words, photographs are indices due to the manner of production: "What is indexical is the mode of production itself, the principle of the *taking*" (Metz 1985: 82). They still possess characteristics of the iconic sign in that "they are in certain respects exactly like the objects they represent." As Calabrese (1986: 723) has put it (and this is the line of thinking that I follow), "We may nevertheless argue that a photograph may also be an icon, for example when it involves portraits, when used for the exhibition of a similarity with a person" (cf. also Tomas' [1983: 26] statement that "the subject's relation to reality is complex. In terms of the production strategy, the subject *is in mimetic relation to the contents of the viewfinder of the camera*; the photograph never relates to the world, but only to the world as defined by the camera's viewfinder—it is a finite world. In terms of tactics, the subject is in iconic relation to the subject in the world, a coding of the subject taking place *before* its impression activates the silver salts of the photosensitive material"). The indexical and iconic aspects, as we will see in considering the "photographs" of Nelson's text, also leave "room for the symbolic aspects as well, such as the more or less codified patterns of treatment of the image (framing, lighting, and so forth) and of choice or organization of its contents" (Metz 1985: 82; cf. also Dubois' [1983: 60-65] treatment of the photograph in terms of the Peircean icon/index/symbol trichotomy).

In applying Peircean semiotic to the theater, we must keep in mind three points. First, as Veltrusky (1964: 84) has indicated, "All that is on the stage is a sign". In the theater, where there is often the attempt to create an impression of a one-to-one representation of reality (as in the photographic image), the icon plays an important role and may lead the observer to the point of losing consciousness of the fact that what is being presented is not the real thing; it is, as Bogatyrev (1976b : 33) has said, "a sign of a sign and not a sign of a material thing." Second, a sign may be iconic, indexical, and symbolic at the same time. Finally, there is an underlying convention controlling the function even of iconic (cf. Eco's "Critique of Iconism," 1976: 191-216) and indexical signs on the stage (cf. Pladott 1982: 31 on indexical signs in the theater: "The difficulty of pinpointing and classifying indexical signs in the theatre is due to the fact that the conventional semantic content ofen precedes the indicating operation"; cf. also Holowka [1984: 69-75] for a general discussion of conventionality and signs). The theater, by its very nature of representation, depends on icons and indices, but as Deely (1985: 34) recently wrote, "The development of theater . . . largely depends on the symbolic dimensions that can be introduced into iconicity."

As various scholars point out in their elaborations on the Peircean concept of sign as a triadic structure of sign in itself, object, and interpretant, misinterpretation can exist, but there is no such thing as a misinterpretant (cf. Short 1981: 199; Ransdell 1977: 172-173, 1986: 683). An understanding of misinterpretation necessarily involves an explanation of Peirce's notion that the sign has two objects:

> It is usual and proper to distinguish two Objects of a Sign, the Mediate without, and the Immediate within the Sign. Its Interpretant is all that the Sign conveys: acquaintance with its Object must be gained by collateral experience. The Mediate Object is the Object outside the Sign. I call it the *Dynamoid* Object. The Sign must indicate it by a hint; and this hint, or its substance, is the *Immediate* object. (Peirce 1977: 83)

The immediate object is the object as it appears at any point in semiosis; it is the object as represented by the sign. As Peirce says, it is "the Object as the Sign itself represents it, and whose Being is thus dependent upon the Representation of it in the Sign" (CP 4.536). The dynamic object (which Peirce also called the Mediate, the Real, and the Dynamoid Object) is the object as it is in itself, independent of what the sign represents it to be; it is the object "as it is regardless of any particular aspect of it, the Object in such relations as unlimited and final study would show it to be" (CP 8.183).

Signs may be false and misleading in that their significance is not what it is taken to be—i.e., something is taken as a sign of something in such a way that the interpretation goes astray. Short (1982: 287) explains that what occurs in false signs is that the immediate objects of the signs "form no part of their dynamic objects" (cf. Buczynska-Garewicz's [1982: 7] observations on the object of the sign, which are of particular interest and applicability to theater semiotics: "According to the fact that no object is present by itself but always is represented by something else, Peirce differentiates between the Real Object, which exists independently of the triadic relationship of mediation, and the Immediate Object, which is presented by sign. Consequently, he concludes that on the level of mediated-by-signs cognition we can never reach the Real Object. No sign gives us pure reality unchanged by interpretation"). An inaccurate or incomplete sign may also lead to misinterpretation; this occurs when the sign is a part of the dynamic object, but does not convey through the immediate object sufficient information about the dynamic object. The immediate object, in other words, does not capture the dynamic object sufficiently to create an accurate sign. Short summarizes the different types of misinterpretation:

> One is where there is no ground that justifies the interpretation: something is taken to be a sign which it is not. Another is where a false or inaccurate sign is taken at face value. In that case the significance of the sign is properly apprehended, but the sign itself ought to be corrected. A third is where an inadequacy goes unrecognized. (1982: 287)

In *Álbum de família*, Nelson Rodrigues works with a similar notion concerning the inability of the sign to capture its dynamic object in all its possible perspectives and angles. The photographic image, which constitutes an essential basis of his play, is a sign that is a static capturing of a "dead" moment of (already past) reality; it cannot capture all the details of reality in its entirety because reality is a live, ongoing, dynamic process. Nelson also exploits the fact that the photograph can create false and inaccurate signs that are often taken at face value.

Throughout the 1940s and 1950s Nelson wrote texts in which there is an obviously strong sense of his role as innovator. In these he turned to various devices and themes that would force his spectator into perceiving common aspects of reality in new and different ways. In *Álbum de família* he accomplishes this by using two items with which his audience would be quite familiar and which they would accept with predictably fixed ideas–the photographic image and the traditional patriarchal family. One he uses as a device which is then raised to the level of content (the photographic image which, as we will see, becomes a point of speculation on reality and illusion and on life and theater); the other exists on the level of content (the patriarchal family, which the author sees as a myth in Brazilian society, in a state of decadence and self-destruction). In this play the dramatist focuses his concern on human perception of the complexities of reality as he deals with the destruction of the mythical patriarchal family, which constitutes one aspect of the text that could be related to a specifically Brazilian context. (There are specific references to Brazilian historical and geographical reality; for example, the Speaker mentions President Artur Bernardes and the Revolution of São Paulo of 1924 in the sixth photograph; there is also the mention of the cities of Belo Horizonte and Três Corações in the state of Minas Gerais, known for its strong sense of tradition and conservatism, in which the patriarchal family would be strong.) However, Nelson uses the family simply as the basic unit of human society. As Cardoso puts it, Nelson

> retrata o estado de decadência da aristocracia e, em particular, a decadência da Família. Mas sua preocupação prioritária não é retratar a famosa patriarcal família, com riqueza de detalhes, como prova ou reflexo de ideais sociais que abalaram a estrutura desta base celular da sociedade, ou então, revelar transformações históricas que reflitam o comportamento social entre os prota-

gonistas de maior relevo (marido e mulher) e seu relacionamento com os filhos e demais pessoas ligadas a esta importante célula social. Tampouco o aspecto ou enfoque econômico, que motivou a decadência ou o esfacelamento da família, seria o objetivo de N. R., embora todos esses aspectos mencionados não possam ser relegados ao abandono, de maneira alguma, para estudo da obra em questão. O que importa é que fique bem claro que todos os estudos sociais, econômicos, históricos, etc. interessam para o estudo de *Álbum de família*, mas o que diferencia N. R. de todo e qualquer dramaturgo brasileiro, é a maneira insólita, singularíssima com que ele trata o tema *família*, temática esta expressa no próprio título da peça.

. . . .

N. R. interessa-se pela família brasileira, na medida exata em que esta mergulha na família universal, partindo da família particularíssima, nascida da família mitológica ou Cosmogônica, vizinha ou parente muito próxima de famílias divinas. (1981: B14-15)

[portrays the decadent state of the aristocracy and, in particular, the decadence of the Family. But his main concern is not in portraying the famous patriarchal family, with a richness of details, as a proof or reflection of social ideas that shake the structure of this cellular base of society, or then, to reveal historical transformations that reflect social behavior among the most outstanding protagonists (husband and wife) and their relationship with their children and other persons linked to this important social unit. Nor would the economic aspect or focus, which caused the decadence or the destruction of the family, be the objective of N. R., although all these aspects can by no means be forgotten in the study of the work in question. What is important is that it be made quite clear that all the social, economic, and historical studies are interesting for the study of *Álbum de família*, but what differentiates N. R. from all other Brazilian dramatists is the unusual and most unique manner in which he deals with the theme of the *family*, this theme being expressed in the title of the play itself.

. . . .

N. R. is interested in the Brazilian family, in the exact measure to which this family is a part of the universal family, departing from the extremely particular family, born of the mythological or cosmogonical family, close neighbor or relative of divine families.]

The characters are mythic beings, and only as such can they be understood; they are timeless creatures, abstractions, manipulated by the playwright to make his point. He accomplishes this technically on the stage by introducing the notion of photography and contrasting this with the live action of theater.

One of the basic features of the photograph—its fusion of past, present, and future—reaffirms the timeless, mythic status of the family. As Tomas (1983: 11) says, "the temporal context spanning photographic activity implies a fusion of the future and the past by way of the present." The paradoxical sense of permanence and order created by the photograph—i.e., its status as "a secular symbol of eternity" (Tomas 1983: 3)—is achieved by a manipulation of time:

> The 'bridge' of permanence is formed by the *strategic* movement from the present of the production strategy to the present of the viewing strategy. *This movement alienates the present by distorting the future and the past* in terms of a desire formed of the production strategy and the viewing strategy: the present becomes past, the future becomes present, and order is imposed on the natural flux and it is given a permanent form—the photograph. (Tomas 1983: 11-12)

The photograph is a paradox in that it makes a permanent, present image of someone or something absent and past (cf. Tomas 1983: 7ff for a discussion of the photograph as a culturalization and socialization of light and absence achieved by "reconciling their contrariness within its structure"). The paradox inherent in the photographic process and the photograph as end product underscores these aspects of Nelson's concept of reality as an unstable fusion and confusion of oppositions and contrasts. The playwright attempts to reconcile these disparate elements into a coherent and meaningful interpretation which is his theatrical text. On the basic paradox of the photograph Nelson constructs his ironic picture album, in which the family, generally seen as a symbol of permanence and continuity in society, is portrayed in a state of decadence and self-destruction.

The nineteenth-century attitude that the photograph is "[a] perfect transcription of the thing itself" (in Orvell 1980: 62) is an attitude Nelson questions in his text; however, this is simply an aspect of a larger question he addresses in this and other plays: i.e., the question of absolutes, absolute definitions of things, the notion of the real as opposed to the illusory. Nelson plays with his audience's faith in and search for absolutes by making a parody of the photographic image as an absolute copy of the object, an absolute of truth and reality. Nelson's play reflects the artist's concern with presenting the relationship between art and life, between the artistically created object and the object in the real world which it supposedly reflects. When he wrote *Álbum de família*, it seems that Nelson was aware of ideas and questions theoreticians would later pose about the photograph: it is a means of communication, and it carries information, but the question is whether this information is "of a purely representational, or referential, or intellectual order, as was believed for a long time when one spoke of the objectivity of the painting" (Mounin 1986: 722).

Nelson's text and notion of the photograph reveal an early awareness of what Orvell says is an attitude typical of American writers after the 1960s—i.e., the photograph is taken by Nelson to be a point of departure for the examination of the relation between the real thing and the reproduction. Nelson's attitude in the 1940s is much in keeping with that of writers and painters today who, according to Orvell, see "photographic realism—in the sense of an unquestioned correspondence between image and subject—[as] a naive fiction" (1980: 62). The photograph was for Nelson, as it is for contemporary writers, "a base for conjectural analysis, an exercise field for the imagination and for speculation on the relationship between image and real thing" (Orvell 1980: 62). Through the photograph, Nelson achieves the same as Orvell's contemporary writer, who "steps back and considers in his fiction the act itself of reproducing the real thing" (Orvell 1980: 50). He looks at theater through the photograph, that is, he uses one medium as a device for examining another.

There are seven instances in *Álbum de família* (cf. Clark and Garcia 1978: 75 for the significance of the sign of seven in the text) when the action on stage is suspended and 'photographs' of the family members (the major characters of the work) are presented:

1) A photograph of Jonas, the patriarch, and Dona Senhorinha taken January 1, 1900, the day after their wedding; this predates the action of the play by some twenty-four years (Rodrigues 1981b: 55. Subsequent references to the text are to this edition).

2) A photograph of the entire family–Jonas, Dona Senhorinha, and the four children, Guilherme, Edmundo, Nono, and Gloria– taken thirteen years after the first photograph (p. 69).

3) A photograph of Gloria at her first communion (p. 75).

4) A photograph of Dona Senhorinha and her sister Rute (p. 86).

5) A photograph of Nono and Dona Senhorinha. Nono is thirteen years old. The picture was taken the day before he went mad, seven years before the present moment of the text (p. 95; the spectator learns the date of the photograph later from the dialogue–cf. p. 108).

6) A photograph of Jonas; the date is 1924 and it is two days before the present moment of the text (p. 108).

7) A photograph of Edmundo and Heloisa on their honeymoon (p. 114). This is three years before the present moment of the play, as the spectator later learns from the dialogue when Heloisa states that they were married for three years (p. 110).

The 'photographs' are not really photographs; they are not images flashed onto a backdrop or screen on stage. They are, in Peircean terms, iconic representations of photographs (i.e., representations of representations), in that they are composed of the actors, who are seen in the process of posing for a photographer. Contrary to what occurs with the photograph–i.e., the object photographed is absent–the object is present and the photograph is absent. The objects themselves, in other words, are presented rather than a photograph of the objects. The photograph is then a device which Nelson uses to play with the concepts of the real and the illusory –the photograph is not really a photograph, it is the real thing, the absent is really present, etc.–upsetting generally established notions. The photographer, who is a character appearing a number of times throughout the text, assumes the role of the artist, as does the playwright, who creates the illusory (i.e., the fictive), that which simulates but which is not life. This is a typical trait of Nelson's texts in this early period–a character assumes a role structurally similar to that of the playwright or the spectator in the work (cf. the role of Alaide in *Vestido de noiva*, who functions in a manner structurally similar to that of the spectator).

There are two levels of text: the static and the dynamic (not necessarily indicated by two separate physical levels of the stage, but at least by two different spaces in temporal terms, since static and dynamic are never used simultaneously on stage). In a sense, Nelson seems to imply a contrast here between photography and film in his use of the static and dynamic. The still, silent timelessness of the photographic scenes is contrasted to the plurality of images achieved on the dynamic level where movement and the auditory elements of the dialogue unfold in time (cf. Metz 1985: 83). The static, which in reality is an extremely dynamic situation because of the dynamic production and interaction of signs that occur there (as it does when we observe a photograph and our imagination fills in many details not observable on the surface), is where the playwright creates a photographic documentary of specific isolated moments of the family. The family album, as is the case in general of this cultural artefact, is intended to be a type of narrative to chronicle the history of the family. However, as Berger (1980: 51) has noted, photographs do not narrate, and therefore may not preserve meaning; they are simply appearances:

> [U]nlike memory, photographs do not in themselves preserve meaning. They offer appearances—with all the credibility and gravity we normally lend to appearances—prised away from their meaning. Meaning is the result of understanding functions. 'And functioning takes place in time, and must be explained in time. Only that which narrates can make us understand.' Photographs in themselves do not narrate. Photographs preserve instant appearances.

Meaning, as we shall see, emerges from the dynamic, live action which contrasts with and often negates the static level (if we think of the dynamic level in terms of film, Metz's [1985: 85] statement is extremely interesting and apt here: "[F]ilm . . . is destruction of the photograph, or more exactly of the photograph's power and action.")

On the level of the static, one area of the stage is lighted during the photographic scenes to indicate the space of the photographer's studio. The space and time of these scenes are isolated and separated from the rest of the text. Each photograph in the album is composed in essentially the same manner on stage: the subjects to be photographed are posed by the photographer, who then disappears with the camera; there is then a pause in which the subject remains in a frozen, static position (this moment constitutes the photograph itself). During this moment the Speaker's voice is heard commenting on the photograph, giving basic information through the verbal channel which cannot be relayed through the visual (e.g., the dates of each photograph). The spectator, for example, could not possibly know highly significant information such as the date of the first photograph–January 1, 1900, the beginning of the year and the century, which corresponds to the notion of genesis and beginning and the concept of the prototypical and mythical family– from visual indices. The only thing that could aid in establishing a date, though imprecise, would be the clothing, certain conventions of posing characteristic of old photographs (indicated in the written text as "a ênfase cómica dos retratos antigos"–p. 55 [the comic emphasis of old photographs]). The sequence of birth of the children in the second photograph and the temporal sequence of the subsequent photographs are other examples of essential information given by the Speaker. The pose is then broken and light is used to indicate a shift from the photographer's studio at the time of the photographic session to the space of the action of the present moment of the text. The actors resume their roles in the live action, and the kinesic code is foregrounded to establish the contrasts of mobile and immobile which will ultimately reveal the contrast of real and illusory (as we shall see).

The dynamic level is where the playwright creates a living documentary, a narrative, of the same family in a series of specific present moments that take place, for the most part, in spaces associated with the patriarchal family (e.g., the plantation home, the small local church). The dynamic interprets the static and reveals over the course of the play that the signs of the static are incomplete and false. Nelson, in other words, produces two sets of evidence (broadly put, two sets of indices–cf. Johansen and Wiingaard 1982) which the spectator must judge: this judging is only possible through the contrast of the signs operating on each level. The sets of evidence are composed of various signs from differing subsystems of theatrical signs (cf. Kowzan 1968) which function iconically and indexically in creating an illusion that reality is being represented on both levels of the text. A tension develops between the two levels when the spectator realizes that the impression of the family conveyed by one is contradicted by the other. The tension is augmented by the fact that the static is composed of configurations of signs that are generally taken to be exact replicas of their objects–i.e., the photograph, which resembles and indicates its object. As Barthes (1981: 5) says, "A specific photograph, in effect, is never distinguished from its referent (from what it represents), or at least it is not *immediately* or *generally* distinguished from its referent." Barthes, interestingly, is echoing Peirce's comments on the relationship between the photograph and reality: "A photograph . . . not only excites an image, has an appearance, but, owing to its optical connexion with the object, is evidence that that appearance corresponds to a reality" (CP 4.447; cf. also Nuttall [1983: 74], who, in discussing the creation of reality in literary texts, touches on photography: "With photography, while we cannot quite say, 'Nothing appears in the photograph which is not founded securely and intelligibly on features present in the scene photographed', we know nevertheless that the odds are heavily loaded in that direction. Thus, although photographs do not invariably provide conclusive evidence, they are usable and are commonly used as sources of evidence").

Nelson reinforces the supposed iconic representation of the photographs through the verbal discourse of a Speaker, who never appears as a character on stage. The Speaker represents, as Nelson (p. 55) states in his sidetext, "uma espécie de Opinião Pública" [a type of public opinion]. As Magaldi (1981b: 19) says, the Speaker "julga pelas aparências" [judges from appearances]—i.e., he affirms what a person would normally see in each photograph. The Speaker gives incorrect information about the family ("prima por oferecer informações erradas sobre a família"—p. 55 [excels in offering erroneous information about the family]). Two possible readings of the photographic scenes are created within the text: the Speaker's comments constitute one, which is easily seen as a parody, and the actors' dialogue and actions constitute the other, which negates the Speaker's interpretation of the portraits. The verbal discourse and actions of the characters on the dynamic level function iconically and indexically to create a contradiction of what is depicted in the photographic scenes. The spectator is then caught between opposing signs, and is forced into a position of judging the evidence on both levels in order to arrive at some kind of understanding and meaning of the disparate nature of the signs supposedly pointing to the same object. Since the evidence of one level contradicts that of the other, the signs of one must be false and/or inaccurate; for the spectator to understand the text, false and inaccurate signs must be corrected by the end of play, and the only way this can be achieved is by judging the signs against each other within the total context of the work.

The static level of photographic scenes is constructed iconically on two levels: first, the actors create an iconic identity by standing in for characters, then they assume the position of pose to simulate the iconic representation of a photograph (there is, in other words, a posing within a posing, a mask within a mask). Within each photograph there are iconic signs that function indexically to convey information: the combination and positioning of characters within each pose point to family relationships; the costumes indicate time period, age group, and social level; facial expressions indicate certain emotions, etc. Taken as a whole (i.e., as the family photograph album), the poses function indexically as temporal markers, indicating the passing of time as the family members mature and grow older. In a sense, there is an irony structured into the text, with the static poses representing the dynamic flow of time. It is also ironic that the static segments, which represent appearance, also may represent the true state of being of the family in that it is 'dead' or stagnant and not progressing or changing over time. The last photograph of the album—that of Edmundo and Heloisa on their honeymoon—parallels the first, in which Jonas and Dona Senhorinha pose before leaving on their honeymoon. Both portray a young couple just beginning their life together; however, the spectator already knows the situation of Jonas and Senhorinha's marriage, and that Edmundo has left Heloisa. Immediately after the photograph of Edmundo and Heloisa, the spectator also discovers that Edmundo was impotent during the three years of their marriage. The photograph would imply (appearance) a continuation of the family, but on the contrary it indicates the end, a final static state (reality).

The verbal discourse of the Speaker that accompanies each pose represents a type of public opinion, as we have said, commenting on the family as an outsider might perceive them; he sees and knows as much about the family as one would by viewing the photographs of them. This verbal discourse emphasizes what one would expect to see in a photograph, what one normally accepts as 'being', as a true representation of reality—i.e., in Peircean terms, a complete capturing of the dynamic object. The spectator, viewing only the photographic scenes and hearing only the Speaker's comments, would accept these scenes as accurate signs of family unity, harmony, happiness, and growth, as any typical family album is expected to reveal. However, on the dynamic level the spectator is bombarded with signs that contradict the final emergence of any such interpretants. As the action of the story develops on the dynamic level, the signs on the static level are constantly put into question, and it becomes more and more difficult for the spectator to accept them as true and accurate.

As each scene is completed, the characters move into action and interaction with each other, creating in the dynamic segments of the text a living portrait of family relations contrary to that collective picture drawn in the isolated poses of the static segments. As Nelson uses an extreme form to represent the supposed 'being' of the family on one level (icon to create iconic representation in the form of a photograph), he uses an extreme form of deviation from familial norms on the other level to show that this 'being' is 'seeming'–i.e., what appears to be reality in the photographic scenes is changed into simple appearance by the time the text ends. The action of the play is structured around a series of triangular relationships among the family members, each relationship being a sign whose interpretant at first glance brings to mind mythic relationships well exploited in world literature from Greek mythology on. Each relationship is a different sign in itself (sign vehicle), in Peircean terms, referring ultimately to the same object and producing the same interpretants, the most obvious one being the clear connection of this text to classical texts. However, upon more careful contemplation, the relationships in this prototypical family may be read as one sign whose object is the destruction of the family unit. The sameness is captured in the underlying structure of the relationships– i.e., the triangle (see Fig. 1). Each triangle has in common the figure of Jonas the partriarch, in relation to various family members who within the structure lose their individuality as they all come to signify the same thing. The various relations may be visually reduced to a similar form that illustrates the interconnectedness of all the relationships through the figure of Jonas (see Fig. 2).

The family, as suggested by one character, has become enclosed within itself, cut off from the rest of the world, and thus already on its way toward isolation and destruction (which as we see throughout the text is a self-destruction). The state of nonbeing is reflected in the image of the return to the uterus (the passage also captures the sense of opposition that is well established

ÁLBUM DE FAMÍLIA

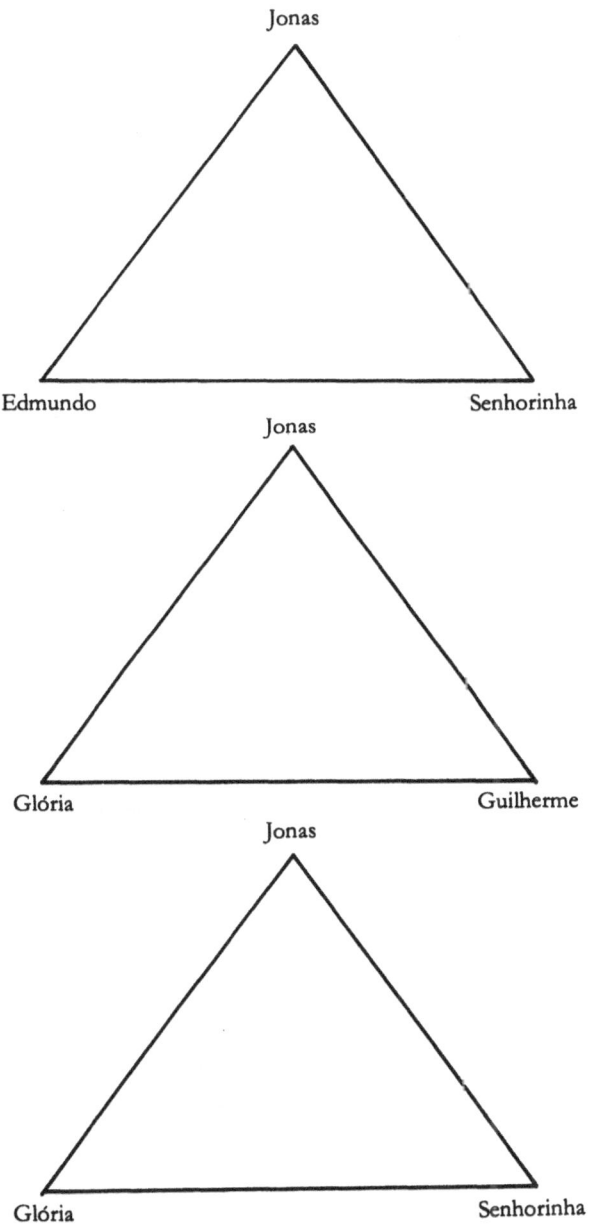

Fig. 1   (Clark and García 1978: 70, 71, 72)

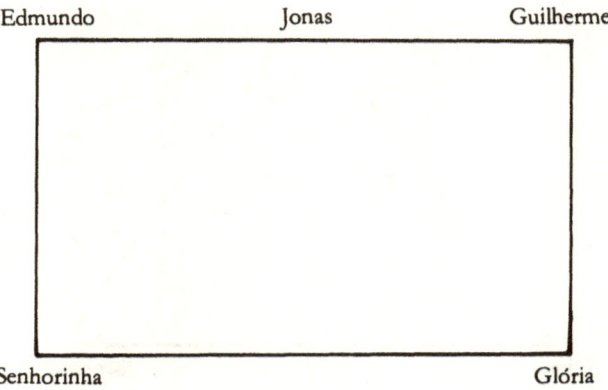

Fig. 2 (Clark and García 1978: 75)

throughout the entire text; here it is being/nonbeing, beginning/ending, construction/destruction, life/death, love/hate):

> EDMUNDO *(mudando de tom, apaixonadamente)*–Mãe, às vezes eu sinto como se o mundo estivesse vazio, e ninguém mais existisse, a não ser nós, quer dizer, você, papai, eu e meus irmãos. Como se a nossa família fosse a única e primeira. *(numa espécie de histéria)* Então, o amor e o ódio teriam de nascer entre nós. *(caindo em si)* Mas não, não! *(mudando de tom)*–Eu acho que o homem não devia sair nunca do útero materno. Devia ficar lá, toda a vida, encolhidinho, de cabeça para baixo, ou para cima, de nádega, não sei. (p. 102)

> [EDMUNDO *(changing his tone of voice, passionately)*–Mother, sometimes I feel as if the world were empty, and nobody else existed, except us, that is, you, Daddy, I and my brothers and sisters. As if our family were the only and the first. *(in a type of hysteria)* Then love and hate would have to be born among us. *(coming to his senses)* But no, no! *(changing his tone of voice)* I think that man should never leave the uterus. He should stay there, his entire life, all cuddled up, with his head pointed down, or up, naked, I don't know.]

This isolation is re-emphasized by the fact that, for the most part, the characters of the text are family members, and there are few outsiders who enter their world. The self-destruction is signified by the negation of the interpretants that are at first generated by the signs of the static segments, where the family is seen in the ordinary family album. The family members, however, are involved in incestuous or potentially incestuous relationship—mother-son, father-daughter, brother-sister—with the accompanying passions of extreme love and/or hate. The result of this web of passions and confusion is the destruction of the family, in the form of self-castration (Guilherme castrates himself so that he will not desire his sister Gloria), suicide (Guilherme kills himself after he kills Gloria; Edmundo shoots himself when he finds out that his mother, who seduces him, had an affair with his brother Nono), sororicide (Guilherme kills Gloria so that Jonas will never possess her), homicide (Dona Senhorinha kills Jonas when he wants to make love to her to produce another female child to be his lover), and insanity (Nono goes insane and lives naked in the woods after making love to his mother). As Sussekind (1977: 13) has stated, "No teatro de Nelson Rodrigues, o que se vê é uma abordagem crítica da estrutura social brasileira, cujo sistema de relações e cujos valores de base tem sua aparente segurança abalada. Para os que violam as regras dessa estrutura as saídas normalmente delineadas em suas peças são a morte e/ou a loucura, ou seja, uma exclusão possibilitada por esse mesmo sistema social" [What is seen in Nelson Rodrigues' theater is a critical treatment of the Brazilian social structure, whose systems of relationships and essential values have their apparent security weakened. The only escape normally described in his plays for those who violate the rules of this structure is death and/or insanity—i.e., an exclusion made possible by the social system itself].

The visual and auditory signs in their iconic and indexical functions in the static segments are not inaccurate or false if isolated and read singularly. Such a reading, however, is not likely because the spectator never really sees the scenes isolated from the context of the entire work. Each of the photographic poses must be taken together within the context of the work created on the dynamic level. There is, however, an irony involved here; the signs of the static 'family album' are accurate in that they are intentionally created and structured into the text by the playwright to function as false and inaccurate in order to force the spectator into correcting them. In other words, Nelson uses familiar signs and 'defamiliarizes' them to offer a new perspective of the object. The spectator is expected to distinguish between simply "seeing" and "interpreting" (as he is expected to confront reality as something complex, demanding more than simply seeing), a notion which Wittgenstein proposes in relation to the photograph (cf. Evans 1978: 230: "[W]e may not be able to see in a picture what we could possibly read into it by employing an alternative method of application." Evans quotes Wittgenstein on this point: "To interpret is to think, to do something; seeing is a state." Evans adds: "It may be felt that if such effort is absent anywhere it is in viewing a photograph" [1978: 231]). The playwright 'utters' a sign, and it is the function of the utterer in any communicative act to put controls or limitations on the sign so that it can be interpreted, so that the intended meaning can be apprehended. However, the utterer (the playwright in this case) may choose to create a sign which is not to be immediately apprehended. When (as in the case of this text) the spectator does not apprehend the sign immediately, the playwright's purpose has been achieved. In *Álbum de família*, Nelson intentionally creates signs on the stage which he expects the viewer to understand in a particular manner at first, but in another manner later; it is a case of interpretation that is misinterpretation, ultimately turned into a more accurate interpretation. In a sense, the sign, in achieving a misinterpretation, has achieved its goal—the first goal, that is. The final goal is the correction of the misinterpretation, which then leads to a greater understanding of all the signs of the text.

The spectator is then forced to reread the photographs of the family album and renegotiate the meaning of each sign—i.e., to go back to the object of each in order to correct the misinterpretation of the sign, taken at face value. To do this, he must return to the general notion of the photograph, and here Nelson's use of the concept of photography may best be explained using the ideas of Barthes, who in discussing the photograph (which, he says, cannot signify "except by assuming a mask") concludes:

> [T]he photograph's immobility is somehow the result of a perverse confusion between two concepts: the Real and Live: by attesting that the object has been real, the photograph surreptitiously induces belief that it is alive, because of that delusion which makes us attribute to Reality an absolutely superior, somehow eternal value; but by shifting this reality to the past ("this-has-been"), the photograph suggests that it is already dead. (1981: 79)

Nelson uses the photographic scenes on stage because people generally accept the photograph as a one-to-one representation of reality. As Bazin (1967: 13-14) has pointed out, the photograph has created a particular psychology in which credibility is central:

> This production by automatic means has radically affected our psychology of the image. The objective nature of photography confers on it a quality of credibility absent from all other picture-making. In spite of any objections our critical spirit may offer, we are forced to accept as real the existence of the object reproduced, actually *re*-presented, set before us, that is to say, in time and space. Photography enjoys a certain advantage in virtue of this transference of reality from the thing to its reproduction.

Nelson questions this credibility, which seems to have been reflected in the notion of reality as portrayed on the Brazilian stage in the early decades of this century—a notion associated with realism which also predominated among North American writers of the 1920s and 1930s. Orvell describes it as "the centrality of the camera as a model for realism: the camera cannot lie" (1980: 55; cf. also Evans 1978: 232: "It has been thought in some quarters that too much attention has been paid to this role [i.e., the photograph as an exact copy of nature] by photographers because of the remarkable powers of reproduction of details possessed by the medium and that the photograph as a vehicle of expression has been neglected"). 'Pictures don't lie', and as Barthes says, they lead one to believe that the object is alive and real and captured in its entirety. Thus, the photograph has an eternal value (Tomas' "secular symbol of eternity" [1983: 3]). Nelson, by contrasting the static with the dynamic (that which is alive and moving—in this case the characters in their family relationships), forces the spectator to realize that the reality of the photograph must be questioned. The photograph as a symbol of "order and permanence" ("As a gesture of possession, reconstruction, and preservation, it is a memory aid; as a collective message, it brings order by way of permanence"–Tomas 1983: 3) is questioned as the photographs are constantly negated throughout *Álbum de família*. Nelson, by showing the falseness of the "order of permanence" (Tomas 1982: 6) achieved through photographic activity, questions the notion of any definable permanence or order in human reality.

The viewer of the performance is compelled to rethink the photograph in terms of what is captured within it. In view of the action of the play, the question emerges: do the photographs present any truth about the family, other than physical appearance at specific times in the past? By the end of the play, the signs of the verbal discourse, coupled with the signs created by the interaction of the characters, reveal that the present is not much different from the past: the feelings, and thus the potential for the incestuous relationships of the present, were always there to be realized. The spectator, then, comes to realize that the photographs do not capture the full reality of their subjects (i.e., the dynamic object). The signs of the static moments are inaccurate because they present only a fragment of the dynamic object; the frozen, dead moment of the past seen in each is only a surface at best, a visual pose, a 'seeming' which is corrected as the living, 'being' actions of the present occur. The falseness of the photographic signs emerge through the indexical functions within each (the facial expressions, the combination of characters, the positioning of each), which suggest marital harmony, family closeness, childish innocence, happiness, etc. over the years as the family grows. Within the context of the play, however, these interpretations are obviously false. They are signs intentionally created to create interpretants that are false signs. The immediate object, in other words, forms no part of the dynamic object. Thus, the photographs, in this sense, as perceived by spectators, are signs with different objects (i.e., their objects appear to be something they are not or, as Ransdell [1986: 676] would say, "an interpretant is being thought of in relation to the wrong sign and/or wrong object"); the signs obviously refer to something else—in this case the deviant family relationships, the strong emotions of love and hate that lead to the destruction of the family. However, what Nelson ultimately captures in his text is the paradoxical human attitude toward the photograph— i.e., that, as Eco says, "A photograph can lie. We realize that, even when we assume, naively, if not under the influence of a fideistic attitude, that it does not" (1984: 223). The photographs become the fiction, and what would generally constitute the fiction of the text (i.e., the dynamic movements of actors and actresses on the stage, involved in dialogues and action) is transformed into fact, into the real of the situation within the textual world.

The correction of the signs on the static level and the accommodation of these within the total sign that is the text can only be achieved through the symbolic function. As Ransdell reminds us, "it is not only possible for the same sign to be at once a symbol, an index, and an icon . . . it is even possible for it to refer to the same object in all three ways at once" (Ransdell 1986: 688). The iconic and indexical functions of each level do not disappear; indeed, the symbolic could not exist if these did not. There is simply a reordering of the hierarchy of sign function: the symbolic emerges in its role of synthesizer, bringing together the function of iconic and indexical and creating a new sign that corrects the false and inaccurate aspects of these functions on the static level of the play. In this synthesis lies the total sign the text comes to represent, that sign which is the sum total of all the signs that compose it.

The symbolic function is underlined by the notion of convention and nonmotivation; this function would not create the particular interpretants it does outside this particular context. In other words, a series of photographs would not normally come to symbolize that which is not real, that which is false and/or inaccurate, just as the actions on the dynamic level would not come to have their particular significance of being the 'real' in contrast to the 'false' outside the context of the fictive world created in this specific dramatic work. It is through the context that the symbolic emerges and synthesizes two disparate elements into a totality that generates meaning.

The work itself becomes a sign in itself of what the playwright considers reality to be (i.e., what he tries to convey to the viewer as reality): neither the static nor the dynamic, but rather a synthesis of the two, one always correcting the other when one does not reveal sufficient information or when one is misinterpreted completely. The dynamic object of the sign (the work) is composed of both being and seeming; the object of the photograph seems to be something, which it may not be, or the photograph seems to be something which it is, but this something is much greater than what the visual image alone can capture. Correction of misinterpretation of signs in the text here is, in a sense, a sign of human existence itself: correction consists of the shifting (and often the reversal) of meaning of signs that occur in man's life, and man must constantly read and reread the signs around him. This is existence, this is making the best of it.

In *Álbum de família*, then, the spectator is shown that which is perceived as real and correct—namely, the photographic representations of the family as a unit, in harmony and growth— and then he is shown something even more real which contrasts with this other reality. There is thus established a contrast of 'being' and 'seeming', and the question emerges: how does one determine being in what seems? The spectator is led to conclude over the course of the play that neither one nor the other completely captures reality, but that reality captures them—i.e., reality is composed of both 'being' and 'seeming'—and that reality consists of the human being's eternal attempts to distinguish one from the other; each person's perception differs from that of the other, thus creating eternally multiple possiblities of reality. The photograph becomes a sign of reality as Nelson perceives it and represents it in his text: uncertainty, flux, paradox, irony. He also shows that conventional realism is *not* reality; that realism, like reality, is variable, not fixed or frozen. Nelson attempts to create a more accurate and accommodating concept of realism and reality composed of not only the iconic and the indexical, but also the symbolic function of the sign. In other words, there is more than just seeing on the surface; there is also that which lurks hidden and always in a state of change and flux beneath the surface. Realness, echoing Orvell, "is no longer assumed to be inherent in the various mimetic modes" (1980: 64). Nelson anticipates Orvell's contemporary "realist", who

> in this climate of confusion between fact and fiction, between information and entertainment . . . has lost the anxiety that characterized his predecessors, has lost the anxiety of competing with supposedly "truer" technologies of mechanical reproduction. But he does, through his art, still picture the world in a way that challenges us to see it in all its confusions. (1980: 64)

Nelson uses the photograph and related notions and attitudes of realism and reality to unmask and demystify the traditional patriarchal family, and thus the patriarchal society of which the family is the basic unit. He achieves this destruction through his underlying concern with the real vs. the imagined, and at the same time comments on theater, art, and life.

During the performance the spectator views the composition and construction of each "photograph", and thus the process of construction of the "family album", which is the text itself. What is seen on stage, then, is the process of the text coming into being, its construction. The text, like some of Nelson's other texts and much of twentieth-century theater, is self-reflexive; the photograph is a subtle meta device that achieves this in the text. The photograph as communicative act resembles the theater in that the relationship between picture and viewer is similar to that between stage and spectator. The following statement from Mounin about the photograph may be applied to the theater:

> [T]hrough the operations of the sender on it, the image is never the objective reproduction of the referent (an objective statement), but it is beyond this a subjective interpretation of this referent (an enunciation). For the receiver of the image and within the framework of his culture, there exist many possible interpretations ranging from decoding or unequivocal reading to a strictly personal interpretation based on indices selected by personal preference in the image, this outside or despite the construction the sender wished to be constraining (1986: 722).

The meaning is the constantly emerging work itself in all its possibilities of contrasts, ironies and paradoxes, and process of construction rather than a final, fixed finished product simply presented to the spectator. The meaning is, in other words, perception itself. The playwright uses the general perception of the photographic image to parallel the spectator's usual perception of the world and theater. The case of Nelson's text is well put in Hornby's (1986: 121) general statements about self-consciousness (one of the six types of metadrama he discerns):

> Since drama is always addressing itself to the ways in which society views reality, human perception is a latent theme of *all* drama. Sensing this, the serious playwright in particular moves toward perception as an overt theme, making explicit what is always implicitly in the background. Drama, which is a *means* of peception, turns upon itself and becomes *about* perception.

CHAPTER IV

THE FICTIVE WORLDS OF *ANJO NEGRO*

Nelson Rodrigues wrote seventeen plays before his death in 1980. These texts, which have now been re-edited into four volumes (1981a, 1981b, 1985, and 1989), showed him to be the most innovative and, at the same time, the most polemical Brazilian playwright of the twentieth century. As Pontes (1966: 39-40) has said, "Nelson paga anualmente o preço do escándalo, cada vez que lança peça nova, como um mártir que respondesse às chamas com blasfêmia" [Nelson pays the price of scandal annually, each time he releases a new play, like a martyr who responds to the flames with blasphemy]. Pelegrino (1966) divided Nelson's plays into two general categories, the "mythic" and the "human", while Magaldi, the organizer of the definitive edition of Nelson's theatrical works, has chosen a different set of categories–the "psychological", the "mythic", and the "Cariocan tragedies". Magaldi (1981a: 9), however, points out that his classification is not an absolute, and must be accorded a certain flexibility; a play in one category may reveal characteristics of another category: "As peças psicológicas absorvem elementos míticos e da tragédia carioca. As peças míticas não esquecem o psicológico e afloram a tragédia carioca. Essa tragédia carioca assimilou o mundo psicológico e o mítico das obras anteriores" [The psychological plays absorb mythic elements and elements from the cariocan tragedy. The mythic plays do not ignore the psychological, and touch on the cariocan tragedy. The cariocan tragedy assimilated the psychological and mythic world of the previous works]. However, in Nelson's theater there is a persistent underlying structure that manifests itself, regardless of the specific approach or context in which he chose to present his material, and regardless of how the reader, spectator, or critic chooses to analyze this material (as esthetic object, psychological analysis, social treatment, etc.). This constant, which lends itself well to a semiotic approach, consists of the construct of the opposition of reality and illusion. It reveals the playwright's pervasive interest and preoccupation (indeed, almost obsession) with a complex world and the incessant struggle to find meaning and understanding in the multiplicity of signs that make up man's realities and fictions.

Nelson Rodrigues wrote *Anjo negro* in 1946, but it was not performed until 1948. Its performance was delayed by the censors, as was that of the previous text, *Álbum de família* (written in 1945, performed for the first time only in 1967), probably for the same reasons—the strong insinuation of incest and the obvious disintegration of the traditional family unit. These texts belong to what Nelson described as "teatro desagradável" [unpleasant theater], plays written to provoke a strong response in the audience, to wake the spectator up to realities never experienced: "são obras pestilentas, fétidas, capazes, por si sós, de produzir o tifo e a malária na platéia" (Rodrigues 1949: 18) [they are pestilential and fetid works, capable by themselves of producing typhoid and malaria in the audience]. In addition to the question of incest and the family unit, Nelson also introduced into *Anjo negro* a new element—that of race and racial prejudice in Brazilian society. However, he presents this in a way far removed from the realistic, thesis type of theatrical treatment typical of the Brazilian stage. Rather than a simple presentation and condemnation of racial prejudice, Nelson uses the issue to bring into question basic human values and emotions, and ties these to the ambiguities of perceptions of reality and illusion in human existence and experience. The text, in other words, should be read on two levels or from two different but quite interrelated perspectives: first as a treatment of the black man in a white society, and how he attempts to resolve this problem, to create his own reality and identity through illusion (or fiction); and second as a text in which the plot parallels the creative process itself—i.e., as a text that reflects its own construction by reflecting the process of fiction as it creates the realities of the text.

Critical reaction to the performance and text was mixed; some critics violently condemned the work, while others defended it equally vociferously (as has often been the case with Nelson's theater—cf. Magaldi 1981b: 22). The premiere was directed by

Ziembinski, so it is probable that the same aggressive, innovative qualities that marked his successful staging of Nelson's *Vestido de noiva* in 1943 were in evidence, calling as much attention to the performance text as the bold written text does to itself.

Anjo negro can be taken as an exemplary text of what Nelson's theater in general accomplishes, a questioning in the dramatic space of the human being's perceptions of and attempts to deal with his realities. This is done in a most shocking and innovative manner in terms of content and dramatic technique. The written text will serve as the basis for this analysis, which will attempt to avoid the problem of written text vs. performance text. Larsen's (1985: 258) notion that "Every reading of a *dramatic* text is directed towards a possible performance text, and thus the actual reception" will serve as an underlying principle in my approach. With Nelson's theater such an analysis is perhaps an easier task than with other theatrical works, because he carefully encodes into the text response eliciting devices that operate on the written as well as on the performance level. In the case of *Anjo negro* these include the thematic content itself—the taboo of incest—and alienation devices achieved through scenic elements described in the sidetext (a highly stylized stage with walls that grow in size, for example), the subversion of traditional values of signs (particularly the symbolism of black and white), and the use of the chorus, which functions as a separate world among the worlds created within the text and offers a constant contrast of real and unreal. For example, the members of the chorus do not constitute "real" persons among the characters of the plot (cf. Chaudhuri 1984: 286-287); since the chorus is indexical of a Western theatrical convention it stands out as a device that points to the text as theater rather than as reality. We must keep in mind, however, that even if certain responses are the same in the written and the performance texts, the manner in which they are provoked is different; alternative sign systems come into play in the performance as channels other than the written word are employed. Elam (1980: 30), citing Eco's notion of ostension as the most basic form of signifying in the performance, says: "Semiotization involves the *showing* of objects and events (and the performance at large) to the audience, rather than describing, explaining or defining them."

In this analysis, the focus is on the various worlds (illusory realities) of the text: first, the fictional world the playwright presents on stage with his characters, and second, the illusory worlds constructed within this primary fictional world by the character Ismael. The first world he creates for himself and his wife Virginia; when it crumbles, he creates another for his stepdaughter Ana Maria and himself, and then he creates a final one in which he plans to enclose himself and Ana Maria forever, but which also fails. The first part of this study will deal with the contents of the text, the worlds as seen in the dialogue and actions of the play; the second part will treat the visual aspect–the setting, props, costume, etc.–that underscore and confirm the notions elaborated in the created worlds.

The approach will draw on aspects of Peirce's semiotic–specifically its basis in the triadic notion of the sign and the concept that "the sign is . . . a basic unit of cognition. And thought has its only existence in signs" (Buczynska-Garewicz 1982: 5). Peirce's theory of semiotic is a theory of communication and epistemology; it deals with problems of human thought and cognition, the entire range of perceptions of the world. Nelson Rodrigues, in his dramatic texts, examines in theatrical, artistic form the same basic questions. In *Anjo negro*, he achieves this through a meta-situation of created worlds within a created world he sets up in the work; the worlds in the text reflect the creation of the text itself, and consequently the entire text becomes a self-reflective sign (i.e., meta-theater). As he is concerned with the process of the spectator–his coming into knowledge of the world around him and then dealing with this knowledge–Nelson shows his characters going through a similar process. In this particular text, however, he has a specific situation worked out in which it becomes obvious that there is a text within the text and that the two parallel each other.

For Peirce nothing is self-given; the world is known only through signs, through the mediating relation which is the sign. Peirce's sign is a dynamic unit consisting of three elements: the sign in itself (the sign vehicle), the object (the referent), and the interpretant (another sign that interprets the sign in itself). As he says, "A sign, or *representamen*, is something which stands to somebody for something in some respect or capacity. It addresses somebody, that is, creates in the mind of that person an equivalent, or perhaps a more developed sign. That sign which it creates I shall call the *interpretant* of the first sign. The sign stands for something, its object" (CP 2.228). Interpretation of the world through signs also implies the concept of misinterpretation. This aspect of Nelson's theater will emerge through study of the similarities and differences of real world vs. fictional world within the fictional world itself. In the final analysis perhaps Nelson perceives no great difference between the real world and theater—one is as real or as illusory as the other, but they are never exactly the same.

Signs have their particular meanings, producing specific interpretants within a culture and a society. These same signs as esthetic signs in a theatrical work may produce different interpretants, possible only within that context. It is important to keep in mind, as Fischer-Lichte (1982: 52) has noted, that the interpretants resulting from theatrical signs are not always identical to the interpretants produced by the same sign outside the text: "The fact should be considered that the meanings of theatrical signs are not always to be identical with the meanings of the signs in the corresponding cultural systems. For as aesthetic signs, theatrical signs have an increased variability of meaning as compared to their corresponding non-aesthetic signs" (cf. also Kowzan 1968: 60: "The theatrical art uses signs drawn from all the manifestations of nature and all human activities. But once used in the theatre each of these signs acquires a significative value much more pronounced than in its original use"). Nelson Rodrigues seems to be well aware of this fact, and even exploits the theater to make the point that human beings tend to assign values fixedly and positively to signs. This results in difficulty in dealing with a reality which is essentially a complex of realities composed of signs with constantly shifting interpretants dependent on such factors as circumstances, context, and individual perception. The shifting interpretant often causes fixed ideas in an individual to be subverted or negated; he is then faced with the problem of having to compromise between what seems to be and what is, what should be and what is. As did Brecht, Nelson exploits "the arbitrariness of the sign, drawing attention to its own artifice rather than attempting to conceal it" (Culler 1983: 53). By constantly reminding the spectator that "this is theater", Nelson constantly reminds him of the distinction between sign vehicle and interpretant, that it is impossible to assign fixed values and meanings to a sign. The sign is in a sense always a signifier in search of a signified, because the signified will always become a new signifier. In Peircean terms, the sign is always in search of an interpretant because the interpretant is a sign that needs an interpretant.

Anjo negro is a play in which little action occurs in the conventional sense; the focus is on the conflicts of the characters, who are more mythic structures (as are the conflicts themselves) than flesh and blood beings of the world. Nelson (1949: 20) recognizes this when, in a response he wrote to some of the criticisms of the text, he says that Ismael does not exist in the world, but that he does live on the stage:

> O caso de Ismael foi interessante. Alegou-se, por exemplo, que não existia negro como Ismael. Entre parênteses, acho que existem negros e brancos piores do que Ismael. Mas admitamos que a acusação seja justa. Para mim, tanto faz, nem me interessa. "Anjo negro" jamais quis ser uma fidelíssima, uma veracíssima reportagem policial. Ismael não existe em lugar nenhum: mas vive no palco. E o que importa é essa autenticidade teatral.

> [The case of Ismael was interesting. It was alleged, for example, that there existed no black like Ismael. Parenthetically, I believe that there exist blacks and whites worse than Ismael. But let's admit that the accusation is fair. For me, it makes no difference; it does not interest me. "Anjo negro" never attempted to be extremely faithful, extremely veracious police reporting. Ismael does not exist anywhere: but he does exist on the stage. And this theatrical authenticity is what matters.

The work is the story of the tortured relationship of Ismael, a black man, and his white wife, Virginia. In Act I, Quadro II (Rodrigues 1981b: 136-146; subsequent references to the text are to this edition), Virginia explains how this unusual union based on revenge, lust, and violence came to be. Virginia, who was an orphan living with her aunt and cousins, was seen kissing the boyfriend of one of the cousins. The boyfriend fled and never returned. The cousin committed suicide, and the aunt, to get her revenge, gave Virginia to the black Ismael to rape ("Deixe que ela grite, deixa ela gritar" —p. 144 [Let her scream, let her scream] she tells Ismael). Ismael bought the house of the aunt, who left with her daughters, and married Virginia thirty days later. From that moment he began to construct a special world of his own; he surrounded the house with walls ("Ele cercou tudo. Muro por toda parte. Para ninguém entrar."–p. 127 [He enclosed everything. Walls everywhere. So that nobody could get in]). He abandoned his successful medical practice and enclosed himself and Virginia in the house where the only others allowed to enter were a maid and the aunt and cousins who came each time a black child was born and died. The world which Ismael constructs is a place where he tries to be what he cannot be: white. He has always wanted to be white: "Desde menino, ele tem vergonha; vergonha, não: ódio da própria cor" (p. 141) [He has been ashamed since he was a child; ashamed, no: he has hated his own color]. Ismael himself admits this later in the text: "Sempre tive ódio de ser negro. Desprezei, e não devia, o meu suor de preto . . . Só desejei o ventre das mulheres brancas . . . Odiei minha mãe, porque nasci de cor . . . "(p. 161) [I always hated being black. I despised my black sweat, and I should not have . . . . I only desired the womb of white women . . . . I hated my mother because I was born black . . . .]. He has worked toward this impossible (in terms of reality) goal, changing certain habits and eliminating certain objects he considers to be signs of blackness

> Quando ele era rapaz, não bebia cachaça porque achava cachaça bebida de negro. Nunca se embriagou. E destruiu em si o desejo que sentia por mulatas e negras . . . (p. 141)
>
> [When he was a young man, he did not drink white lightning because he thought that it was a drink for blacks. He never got drunk. And he destroyed in himself the desire that he felt for mulattas and black women . . .]
>
> Tirou da parede o quadro de São Jorge, atirou pela janela—porque era santo de preto (p. 142)
>
> [He took the image of St. George off the wall and threw it out the window—because he was a saint for blacks]

He had studied to be a physician because this profession was a sign of whiteness to him.

The isolation Ismael creates for himself and Virginia is a world where he attempts a new beginning. It is a striving for an undifferentiated space where there is no person for Virginia to see but him. Black can cease to be black and he can be what he wishes. In Act I, Quadro I (pp. 125-136) the dialogue between Virginia and Ismael indicates the success that he has had in creating his fiction, his illusory world:

O mundo está reduzido a nós dois—eu e você (p. 132)

[The world is reduced to the two of us—you and I]

O mundo reduzido a mim e a você, e um filho no meio—um filho que sempre morre (p. 133)

[The world reduced to me and you, and a child in the middle—a child that always dies]

Já me esqueci dos outros homens, já sinto como se no mundo só existisse uma fisionomia—a sua—todos os homens só tivessem um rosto—o seu (p. 133)

[I've already forgotten other men, I feel as if there were only one look in the world—yours—as if every man had only one face—yours]

Virginia has a vague memory of the face of another man and only after great difficulty remembers that it is the face of Jesus; she begs for a picture of Jesus, but Ismael denies her this. No other face can enter this world; it would create difference, and Ismael would have to return to his state of blackness and all the associated signs of inferiority. Ismael relates in this scene how and why he created this special world, this special reality:

> Se eu quis viver aqui, se fiz esses muros; se juntei dinheiro, muito; se ninguém entra na minha casa—é porque estou fugindo. Fugindo do desejo dos outros homens. Se mandei abrir janelas muito altas, muito, foi para isso, para que você esquecesse, para que a memória morresse em você para sempre . . . . Virgínia, olha para mim, assim! Eu fiz tudo isso para que so existisse eu. Compreende agora? Não existe rosto nenhum, nenhum rosto branco!—só o meu, que é preto . . . . (p. 134)

> [If I wanted to live here; if I had these walls made; if I saved money, lots of it; if nobody comes into my house—it's because I'm fleeing. Fleeing the desire of other men. If I had high windows put in, very high, it was for this, for you to forget, for your memory to die forever . . . . Virginia, look at me, like this! I did all this so that only I would exist. Do you understand now? No other face exists, no white face!—only mine, which is black . . . .]

What Ismael has tried to do in this world he has created corresponds to what Peirce calls Firstness in his definition of the phenomenological categories, the basis of his semiotic. In these Peirce discerns three levels of being or modes of experience —Firstness, Secondness, Thirdness—which "explain the essential nature of signs and ground the inherent structure of the sign universum" (Buczynska-Garewicz 1983: 316). The description of the sign is begun with a description of the categories present in any sign. Peirce defines Firstness as the "mode of being of that which is such as it is, positively and without reference to anything else" (Peirce 1977: 24), and he says that it is the state of being in which things are "what they are regardless of anything else" (CP 1.295). It is, in other words, that state of being in which there is no comparison of one element with another, no differentiation of one from the other. It is "an instance of that kind of consciousness which involves no analysis, comparison or any process whatsoever, nor consists in whole or in part of any act by which one stretch of consciousness is distinguished from another" (CP 1.306). The sign vehicle is a First; it is a possibility which, until it enters into the triadic relationship of the sign, remains a potential sign. It is void in that it does not represent anything until it enters the mediating triadic relationship and represents something to somebody. A sign vehicle is a "First which stands in such a genuine triadic relation to a Second, called its *Object*, as to be capable of determining a Third, called its *Interpretant*" (CP 2.274). Firstness, then, is that mode of being in which there are signifiers which are not yet connected with signifieds— there are no signs, only possibilities. This is the level of being—Edenic in a sense, a place of purity where desires do not enter—which Ismael attempts to create in the world he constructs for himself and Virginia (it is interesting to note that Peirce [CP 1.357] described Firstness in terms of Adam: "What the world was to Adam on the day he opened his eyes to it, before he had drawn any distinctions, or had become conscious of his own experience— that is first, present, immediate, fresh, new, initiative, original, spontaneous, free, vivid, conscious, and evanescent").

Sign vehicles are only potentials that can be manipulated. This is what Ismael wants to do: assign meanings arbitrarily to signs to suit his own purpose. He wants to create a place in which there is no differentiation between black and white. In such a place he could see himself as he wishes to be seen by others: white. However,

Ismael cannot succeed because the perfect beginning cannot be created. Virginia already has knowledge of the world, and this cannot be erased. Peirce explains, "there is but one state of mind from which you can 'set out,' namely, the very state of mind in which you actually find yourself at the time you do 'set out'—a state in which you are laden with an immense mass of cognition already formed, of which you cannot divest yourself if you would" (CP 5.416). The possibilities Ismael wishes to create, sign-vehicles devoid of meaning, have already existed in reality (Secondness) for Virginia. Secondness is "an occurrence... something that *actually*—takes place" (CP 7.538). It "is the category of the *actual existent*... Seconds are unique existences, unique in time and space" (Zeman 1977b: 24). Virginia has lived, she has a past; as Peirce remarks, "we may say that the bulk of what is actually done consists of Secondness —or better, Secondness is the predominant character of what *has been done*" (CP 1.343). For Virginia, black is already a defined visual sign (Thirdness) with specific racial and emotional implications. A sign is a representation relation, a Third. As Peirce says, "any mentality involves thirdness" (Peirce 1977: 29), which is "the triadic relation existing between a sign, its object, and the interpreting thought, itself a sign, considered as constituting the mode of being a sign" (Peirce 1977: 31). Gorlée has succintly summarized and contrasted Secondness and Thirdness: "[I]t is through Secondness that we face reality and in the process acquire experience" (1987: 46), and "Thirdness permits us to make sense of a reality which does not advance unequivocal meaning" (1987: 47).

Another factor accounts for the failure of the first world Ismael attempts to create: the unexpected entrance of his blind stepbrother Elias, who brings Virginia closer to reality as it exists outside the walls of the house. Elias is white; Ismael always hated him for this, so when Elias was being treated for eye problems as a child, Ismael switched medications, causing an incorrect and dangerous one to be put in his stepbrother's eyes. Soon after this incident Ismael disappeared from home; Elias has come in search of him to deliver the mother's curse on him. Elias enters in Act I, Scene I, as the dead black baby is to be buried. Ismael allows him to stay in the house with the understanding that he is not to go near Virginia. However, Virginia finds out that he is in the house, and that he is white, and bribes the maid to let her out of her locked room. She seduces Elias, telling him that he could be her salvation from the situation with Ismael, not by helping her to escape but rather by giving her a white child. Thus Ismael's first fiction comes to a close. Virginia has broken out of the enclosure and isolation through Elias. It is not, however, a physical escape; she will have to remain in the house and watch Ismael construct yet another world.

Act III, which takes place sixteen years after the birth of Ana Maria (the child of Elias and Virginia), is Ismael's second attempt at creating his own special world. He has transferred all his feelings from Virginia to Ana Maria, and it is with her that he wishes to create a special world for himself—the world he tried to create for himself and Virginia, one away from whites where he can be white. Ismael takes Ana Maria—who was born white and female, and therefore is of no interest to her mother, who wanted a white male child-lover—and allows her to see no face other than his for months and months. He allows her to hear no other voice at all, then blinds her by putting drops of acid in her eyes. With her visual perception of the world removed, Ana Maria perceives the world, external reality, only through the eyes of Ismael who creates a reality for her through verbal signs. He tells her that he is white, that the rest of the world is black; that he is good, that the rest of the world is evil.

> Sabe que eu fiz isso para que ela não soubesse nunca que eu sou negro. *(num riso soluçante)* E sabes o que eu disse a ela? desde menina? que os outros homens – todos os outros – é que são negros, e que eu –compreendes? – eu sou branco, o único branco *(violento)* eu e mais ninguém. *(baixa a voz)* Compreendes esse milagre? E milagre, não é? Eu branco e os outros, não! Ela é quase cega de nascença, mas odeia os negros como se tivesse noção de cor . . . . (p. 175)
>
> [Do you know that I did that so that she would never know that I am black. *(sobbing and laughing)* And do you know what I have told her? since she was a little girl? that other men—all others—are black, and I–do you understand?—I am white, the only white *(violent)* I and nobody else. *(he lowers his voice)* Do you understand this miracle? It's a miracle, isn't it? I'm black and the others are not! She's been blind almost since birth, but she hates blacks as if she had some notion of color . . . .]

Ismael exploits the arbitrary nature of the sign and creates a reality that corresponds to no other. However, it is not Ismael's reality; he takes part in it only vicariously, through Ana Maria. He participates in an illusory world through a real person (as the spectator participates in an illusory world in the theater through a real person, the actor), but he must also participate in the reality of his own world. Ana Maria cannot visually perceive external reality; it does not exist for her except through the verbal signs of Ismael. It is a reality that only exists in verbal discourse, through verbal signs. She lives in her darkness while the spectator sees the falseness of her existence.

Ismael is caught up in the traditional symbolic values of black and white in his society, in the pretextual world previous to his artificially fabricated worlds, where black is inferior and white is superior. He desires the impossible—to be white in a society where white is the dominant racial color. The playwright, however, questions and challenges these traditional assignments of value and subverts them, upsetting audience expectations while creating new possibilities and potentials for black and white as signs within the society of his spectators. His spectators, usually of the white middle and upper classes, would associate black and white with particular values within that society on the basis of traditional racial values, and also traditional Western, Christian values. Black and white, in other words, are not only signs of specific races, but also of the emotional values of good and evil. However, black and white become interchangeable within the context of the textual world. This is achieved on two levels: in the world created by the playwright and in the world Ismael creates for Ana Maria. We will return later to the author's created world with a discussion of the physical stage and the setting, but for the moment, we will examine this reversal of signs within Ismael's created world.

Ismael subverts the traditional significations of black and white by making Ana Maria believe that he is white and the rest of the world is black. He can do this because she is blind and therefore colors exist for her only through verbal signs; these do not have referents in the world beyond the walls of the house. When Virginia tries to convince her that Ismael is not her father and that he is black, Ana Maria's reponse is a violent one: "Preto, meu pai? (*feroz*) Ele, não. Os outros, sim. É por isso que ele me esconde aqui, que me guarda, não deixa ninguém falar comigo, a não ser você. Porque todos são pretos, (*repete, espantada*) todos! Até no livro que meu pai leu para mim" (p. 182) [Black, my father? (*fierce*) He's not. The others are. It's because of that he hides me here, that he protects me and does not let anybody except you talk to me. Because all of them are black, (*frightened, she repeats*) all of them! Even in the book that my father read to me...]. The truth of the signs, in terms of the world outside the house, has never been challenged, until the moment Virginia confronts her daughter with the external reality. The physical conditions of Ana Maria's world are analogous to those of her mother and father–the isolation of the house with its high walls. However, the darkness that pervades the house ("A casa não tem teto para que a noite possa entrar e possuir os moradores" –p. 125) [The house does not have a roof so that the night can enter and possess the inhabitants] is doubled in her case by blindness.

As Scott (1983: 159) has noted, "Peirce regarded semiosis as the process by which reality is revealed. The sign-object-interpretant relation of his particular theory is intended to describe the form of this process. Reality (the object) becomes manifest through the mediation of signs, and these signs are apprehended or responded to (the interpretant)." In *Anjo negro* the spectator observes the various realities revealed by the representation relation. Ismael has changed the usual objects through manipulation of signs. In the world he creates for Ana Maria, his reality–that he is black, not white–is not revealed to her. Ismael has created referents (objects) for the verbal signs of black and white which are the reverse of what is real for the spectator. However, this does not mean that what Ana Maria possesses is not also real. The sign is arbitrary, and it does not matter whether something is called black or white as long as there is agreement among the users of the signs. Her interpretants are indeed interpretants; there is no such thing as a misinterpretant, but misinterpretation does occur and this is a prime example of it. The signs that have been created for Ana Maria have, as Short (1982: 287) would say, "significance or grounded interpretability, yet what they signify is not. That is, their immediate objects form no part of their dynamic objects." The immediate object is "the world, or some portion of it, *as* the sign represents it to be," and the dynamic object is "the world, or this portion of the world, as it really is–that is, as it is independently of what it is represented to be" (Short 1982: 286). Ana Maria is the only person in her world; the meanings of the signs of black and white Ismael has formulated are not the meanings that exist for those signs in his world. Reality for Ana Maria is illusion for Ismael, as it is for the spectator. Ana Maria's interpretants do not mediate between the same objects and sign vehicles as do the signs for Ismael and the spectator. There are two different semiotic sequences involved here (cf. Scott 1983: 159).

Ismael succeeds in misinterpretation with Ana Maria. She refuses to believe Virginia when the latter says that Ismael is not Ana Maria's father and that he is not white. Ismael arbitrarily assigns meanings to signs; he shows his stepdaughter only his face and then blinds her. Later, when she can understand language, he tells her that he is white and that he is her father. He has turned himself into two false signs: father and white. To the spectator and to himself, he is neither, but to Ana Maria he is both. His illusion becomes her reality, in which he participates through her. For Ana Maria he has reduced the original symbols (the symbols of black and white and the symbol of father) to potentials. In terms of interpretants, signs at this level are rhemes, interpretational possibilities of signs. The rheme "is any sign that is not true or false" (CP 8.337). As Pinto (1989: 44) explains, "a rheme is a sign whose interpretant is not limited in that to which it can refer as its object; that is, it is an open, indeterminate sign in the sense that its interpretant contains at least one unbound variable, as in 'X hits the wall' or 'X hits Y'." Ismael converts these traditional symbols into rhemes, then dicentalizes (a dicent is "a sign *capable* of being asserted" [CP 8.337]) them by assigning new meanings to them, thus allowing the emergence of unexpected arguments (white is superior and good, black is inferior and evil; I am white, therefore I am good and superior to all others in the world, because the world is made up of blacks and they are evil). This, however, is possible only within the world of Ana Maria, within the artificial construct of signs Ismael has built for her. It is the same type of world that he wanted for himself and Virginia, a world in which only she and he existed and where he could create signs and meanings. With Virginia this did not work because another world of signs and meanings already existed for her; what was left of Ismael's first artificial world was finally destroyed by the intrusion of Elias. The world of Ana Maria was created from a pure beginning, from the point where she had no "mass of cognition already formed". It was then maintained not only by physical enclosure but also by her blindness, the loss of her visual perception of the world around her. Ismael reduced her to almost total dependence on him for her perceptions of the world.

Within this world Ismael subverts traditional signs and values, causing the spectator to question his own perceptions and to view things in a different light. At the same time the playwright subverts the same signs within his total fictional world of the stage. The spectator, who accepts the same symbolic meanings of black and white as all the characters of the play except Ana Maria do, begins to see that the traditional association of black with evil and white with good does not exist within the world of the text. The spectator is forced into reassessing his understanding of these signs as certain events unexpectedly occur to cause him to question the traditional meanings. Ismael, whose presence looms over that of Virginia, is by the end of the play no longer seen as the evil black man who repeatedly rapes the innocent white Virginia. The image of Virginia's innocence and goodness begins to crumble in Act II, Scene I, where the spectator learns that she has killed her three babies because they were black; in the same scene she uses Elias for her own purpose of revenge. The spectator's expectation that Virginia in all her whiteness represents purity and innocence is further subverted by the revelation that Virginia's plan was to have a white male child by Elias so that she could eventually have a white lover in the house ("sinto que amarei teu filho, não com amor de mãe, mas de mulher"–p.167 [I feel that I will love your son, not as a mother but as a woman]; "como mulher, ou como fêmea"–p. 173 [like a woman or like a whore]). In Act III the spectator also learns that Virginia hates her daughter and has always considered her to be an enemy ("Mas quero que saibas que menti quando disse que te amava . . . "–p.185 [But I want you to know that I lied when I said I loved you . . .]; "Você foi sempre minha inimiga"–p. 186 [You were always my enemy]).

Virginia establishes the contrast between Elias and Ismael early in the text in terms of white/black, good/evil, and innocent/corrupt, and thus draws the spectator into believing she is the opposite of her husband and that she suffers a life of torment. In Act I, Scene II, in her first encounter with Elias, she speaks of her hatred (although with uncertainty in her voice) of Ismael; she expresses her disgust for him in terms of the smell of sweat and how it permeates the house and her body, thus emphasizing her entrapment by him: "Se eu gosto dele? Não . . . não gosto . . . (*incerta*) Odeio . . . A transpiração dele está por toda a parte, apodrecendo nas paredes, no ar, nos lençóis, na cama, nos travesseiros, até na minha pele, nos meus seios, meu Deus!" (p. 142) [Do I love him? No . . . . I don't love him . . . . (*unsure*) I hate him . . . . His sweat is everywhere, rotting in the walls, in the air, in the sheets, in the bed, in the pillows, even in my skin, in my eyes, on my breasts, my God!]. In Act III she tells Ana Maria that her dead father, Elias, is the pure, innocent being: "Ele poderia possuir a mim, ou qualquer mulher, e não haveria pecado—nenhum, nenhum! O corpo ficaria mais puro do que antes" (p. 181) [He could possess me or any woman, and it would not be a sin—not at all! The body would be purer than before]. The spectator, although he already has reason to suspect that Virginia and Ismael do not represent a clear example of good vs. evil, is caught off guard in Act III, Scene II when Virginia openly enters into competition with Ana Maria for Ismael ("Ele é meu, não teu . . . "[185]). Is Virginia lying when she tells Ismael that she loves him and that she has always loved him, or is she simply competing with her daughter because she hates Ana Maria? The spectator cannot really decide. Virginia herself does not know, and the line between love and hate is a thin one in this world. It is as difficult to define these terms as it is to specify exactly what is real and what is illusion for the characters. However, in the final act the spectator becomes aware that there is little or no difference between Virginia and Ismael; they are almost the same being, a being in which the battle of black and white as symbolic of evil and good exists. Virginia would have done the same thing with a white son that Ismael has done with Ana Maria; she would have taken her son as a lover and constructed a special world in which only she would exist for him:

> . . . eu o tomaria para mim, só para mim; não deixaria que ninguém—nenhuma mulher—surgisse entre nós. Eu e ele criaríamos um mundo tão pequeno, tão fechado, tão nosso, como uma sala . . . Como uma sala não! Como um quarto . . . (*eufórica*) Nada mais que este espaço, nada mais que este horizonte—o quarto (p. 173).

> [. . . I would take him for myself, just for me; I would not let anyone—no woman—come between us. He and I would create such a small world, so closed, so ours, like a living room . . . . Not like a living room! Like a bedroom . . . . (*euphoric*) Nothing more that this space, nothing more than this horizon—the bedroom.]

Virginia and Ismael are reduced to the same level in their already reduced world.

Ismael's world with Ana Maria is to be completed by a final act. He allows Virginia to spend three nights with Ana Maria trying to convince her that he is not her father, that he is not white, and that he is evil. During that time he builds a glass mausoleum to enclose himself and Ana Maria away from Virginia (whom he has ordered from the house) and the rest of the world. The glass tomb will be a tomb within the tomb that is the house. The final enclosure, the ultimate isolation and most complete separation of Ismael from the world in which he can only be black, is possible only through the final reality of death. However, the destruction of Ismael's and Ana Maria's private world comes through Virginia, who seduces him away from her daughter. Ismael realizes that Ana Maria only loves him because she thinks that he is white; he realizes that the illusory world he has created around Ana Maria is not his own: "Só me ama porque menti–tudo o que eu disse a ela é mentira, tudo, nada é verdade! (*possesso*) Não é a mim que ela ama, mas a um branco maldito que nunca existiu!" (p. 190) [She only loves me because I lied–every thing that I said to her was a lie, everything, nothing was true! (*possessed*) It's not me that she loves, but rather a cursed white man that never existed!]. He must rid himself of her because she will always come between him and Virginia, who now professes to love him because he is black ("Eu te quero preto . . ." –p. 190 [I love you black . . .]). Virginia has the solution, and the two of them entice the blind Ana Maria into the glass mausoleum. In a final act symbolic of the two having been reduced to the same sign, each closes one door of the mausoleum, condemning Ana Maria–the daughter/lover–to death. The two are no longer simply characters; they are symbolic entities referring to the same object, the paradoxical nature of reality. The chorus indicates this sameness of the two as it ends the text with a lament, equating love and hate, Virginia and Ismael:

>SENHORA: O Virgínia, Ismael!
>SENHORA (*com voz de contralto*):   Vosso amor, vosso ódio não tem fim neste mundo!
>TODAS (*grave e lento*):   Branca Vírginia . . .
>TODAS (*grave e lento*):   Negro Ismael . . . (p. 192)

[SENHORA: Oh Virginia, Ismael!
SENHORA (*in a contralto voice*): Your love, your hatred have no end in this world!
ALL (*austere and slow*): White Virginia . . .
ALL (*austere and slow*): Black Ismael . . .]

To the spectator, the created worlds of the text are portrayed through auditory and visual channels. Actors engage in dialogue amid objects on stage which serve within the semiotic systems of the theatrical code. The theater is a conjunct of multiple signs and sign systems, in which one sign system often takes over for another or works with that system to reinforce the signifying process (cf. Elam's [1980: 72-76] discussion of this phenomenon, which he calls "transcodification"). In *Anjo negro*, the visual underscores the verbal, and at times the verbal must perform part of what the visual would normally accomplish. For example, the darkness that pervades Ismael's house, according to the instructions of the playwright ("A casa não tem teto para que a noite possa entrar e possuir os moradores"–p. 125 [The house has no roof so that the night can enter and possess the inhabitants]; "A noite cai, contra todos os relógios, porque há ainda sol em outros lugares; é, pois, uma noite prematura e triste"–p. 147 [Night falls, contrary to all clocks, because there is still sun in other places; it is then a premature and sad night]), cannot literally exist on stage or the spectator would not be able to see the actors. Darkness must be implied through low lighting and verbal representation. Visual images of Ismael's house are created through the verbal discourse: "Noutras casas, ainda tem sol. Nesta já é noite" (p. 147) [In other houses there is still sun. In this one it is already night]. The same image is created again by the chorus in Act III, along with another example of the verbal conveying information which the visual cannot; the creation of temporal markers: "Há 16 anos que não faz sol nesta casa. Há 16 anos que é noite", (p. 170) [It has been sixteen years since there was sun in this house. For sixteen years it has been night].

The stage setting–essentially only one throughout the text, the house of Ismael–is not the traditional realistic stage. Its purpose is not to convince the spectator to accept the performance as a direct reproduction of a world that exists or has existed. It is more a schematic, symbolic use of stage space, with only a few props that function as signs in a variety of ways to achieve the effects of paradox, opposition, and the play between the real and the illusory. To explain the visualization of the text and how this underscores and emphasizes the verbal code, it will be necessary to discuss another aspect of Peirce's semiotic—the trichotomy that describes the relation between the sign and its object. Peirce defines a number of trichotomies of the sign. Three major ones, based on the relation of the sign to the three elements of the triad, are the foundation of his semiotic: (1) the sign vehicle in relation to itself; (2) the sign in relation to its object; and (3) the sign in relation to its interpretant. These three divisions yield further trichotomies, resulting in sixty-six classes of signs. The most widely used of the three basic divisions, particularly by semioticians of theater, and the most fundamental according to Peirce (2.275), is that of the sign and object, which breaks down into the well-known tripartite model of icon, index, and symbol.

The relation between the iconic sign and its object is grounded on similarity; the icon "has no dynamical connection with the object it represents; it simply happens that its qualities resemble those of that object, and excite analogous sensations in the mind for which it is a likeness. But it really stands unconnected with them" (CP 2.299). The index functions as a sign by pointing to its object; the relation between the sign and its object is causal or contiguous. The indexical sign "is physically connected with its object; they make an organic pair, but the interpreting mind has nothing to do with this connection, except remarking it, after it is established" (CP 2.299). The relation between iconic and indexical signs is an interesting aspect of theatrical sign systems in that the spectator, as Pladott (1982: 36) indicates, tends to see indexical signs as iconic: ". . . while iconicity takes indexical elements, such as gesture, costume, etc., for granted, the viewer tends to see all gestures as iconic." The symbolic function rests on the arbitrary and conventional relation of the sign to its object. In the theater, as in art in general, this sign function is bound to context, and is associated with the esthetic function of the work. The symbolic sign "is connected with its object by virtue of the idea of the symbol-using mind, without which no such connection would exist" (CP 2.299).

In using Peirce's typology of signs to analyze theatrical signs, it is important to keep in mind that a sign may be an icon, index, and symbol all at the same time, and that "it is even possible for it to refer to the same object in all three ways at once" (Ransdell 1986:

688). The concept of hierarchy is important here. Peirce, in his definition of the phenomenological categories, associates the icon with Firstness, the index with Secondness, and the symbol with Thirdness in a hierarchical structure, the higher category always implying the lower one(s). It will be observed in our analysis that most textual signs are all three, but the spectator does not necessarily identify all three at the same time. On the contrary, it is the continually shifting sign function–the tension between the iconic and symbolic–and the foregrounding and backgrounding of one or the other function in the various theatrical sign systems (cf. Kowzan [1968], who identifies and defines 13 such systems) that creates the final interpretant of the sign which the text in itself becomes.

The spectator's initial contact with the stage is a visual one. The space that has been set aside for the performance is a "Cenário sem nenhum carácter realista" (p. 125) [A setting without any realistic characteristics]. It is a highly stylized space where the world of the characters is reduced to a state of enclosure and isolation, and the relationships among them are ultimately reduced to a post-Edenic state of chaos. The reduction of the world to this state signifies Ismael's attempts at order and meaning. However, as portrayed visually on stage by walls that grow higher, and visually and verbally by the night that constantly descends, this order is threatened by chaos. The props are essentially the same throughout except for a baby's coffin in Act I, the glass mausoleum in Act III (different sign vehicles for the same referent–i.e., signs of the death of the children in the family), and the walls at the back of the stage which increase in height as the play progresses ("Ao fundo, grandes muros que crescem à medida que aumenta a solidão do negro"–p. 125 [In the background, high walls that get higher as the black man's solitude increases]). Although the setting is static in that it does not change, the space itself is dynamic for the spectator in that the signs that constitute its being, those signs which the spectator perceives visually as accompaniment to the verbal discourse, are charged with shifting functions, and therefore changing meanings. The dynamic quality results from the shifts in the spectator's perception of the signs as functioning iconically, indexically, or symbolically. The spectator, at an early point in the text, is encouraged to question the purely iconic and indexical (mimetic) nature of the stage signs. As the work develops the house loses its concrete aspect as simply the house of Ismael; it becomes also a symbolic space of isolation and aloneness where the characters, as I have indicated, are more mythical entities or structures than flesh and blood beings involved in everyday actions and events (cf. Clark and García 1978: 79-87). The house becomes a symbolic space charged with interpretational possibilities: psychological, allegorical, mythical, depending on the manner in which the spectator chooses to approach it. The house, like the stage, is a place of creation of illusions which are destroyed when the actors withdraw.

Various contrasts occur on the stage, and the usual interpretants, such as black vs white and evil vs good, lose their traditional meanings and acquire new interpretive dimensions. The contrasts are embodied in the various theatrical sign systems conjoining in the spectacle, which engages the spectator's attention and tests his interpretational abilities. The stage is not totally bare, not totally symbolic, but it tends toward this with its minimal scenic metonymies that function indexically to indicate space. However, the iconic function of the props (including the costumes used for the characters Virginia and Ismael) is threatened by the symbolic, and the spectator is torn between accepting them as real or symbolic or both as he attempts to bring order and understanding to the conjunct of signs that confronts him. The house as represented on the stage consists of two levels: an upper level, which is a bedroom, and the lower level, which is a living room. The bedroom contains two beds, one made and the other in a state of disarray. The levels are connected by a stylized stairway. The lower level, in Act I, is where the wake for the dead child occurs; in Act III it is the location of the glass mausoleum.

The characters themselves, their language, and their costumes add to the setting and the contrasts. As Kott notes, "In the theater the basic icon is the body and voice of the actor" (1969: 19). Pavis adds, "The language of the actor is iconized in being spoken by the actor, i.e. what the actor utters becomes the representation of something supposedly equivalent to it, discourse" (quoted in Elam 1980: 23). The actors' gestures and tone of voice are naturalistic; there are no sustained exaggerations that turn these into symbolic signs. The iconic and indexical functions are not threatened; they simply create a great contrast with the symbolic stage space, and both are synthesized into a sign of paradox, of contrast between real and illusory. The costumes are indexical of a certain social status and certain emotional states. Virginia's black dress is an indication of her state of mourning. However, the contrast in the characters' race and costume will contribute to the tension of sign functions that accompanies the other tensions in the text. Virginia is white ("muito alva"), dressed completely in black. Ismael is black, dressed completely in white.

As the play opens, the spectator views the stark contrast of colors and also a group of black women dressed in black, serving as a chorus. With the chorus Nelson successfully revives a theatrical device that has often been revived in contemporary theater but "has failed somehow to flourish, or flourished only as a literary and archaic device, deprived of the context and ground that in the Greek theatre gave it a natural rightness" (Arrowsmith 1974: 125). The chorus in Nelson's text functions much the same as it did in the Greek theater:

> [T]he chorus attends the action as a dependent society in miniature, giving the public ressonance of individual action. Thus the chorus exults, fears, wonders, mourns, and attempts, out of its store of traditional moralities, to cope with an action whose meaning is both difficult and unfamiliar. By so doing, the chorus generalizes the meaning of the action and at the same time the action revives and refreshes the choral wisdom. But almost never is the chorus' judgement of events authoritative; if it is an intruded voice, it is normally the voice of tradition, not the dramatist. (Arrowsmith 1974: 125)

The chorus does not participate in the action or dialogue of the text. It is independent of the actors and does not figure into the fictive world of the characters. The black women do not speak directly to any one character, nor do they promote the plot in any way. Although its members speak individually, the chorus essentially represents one voice in terms of attitudes and opinions. It observes, moralizes, and prophesies (as in the end of the play when it predicts that Virginia will have another black child that will die like the others: "Em vosso ventre existe um novo filho! . . . Futuro anjo negro que morrerá como os outros!"–pp. 191-2 [There is a new child in your womb! . . . A future black angel that will die like the others]). At the same time it supplies vital information such as temporal markers and details of the plot and setting that are not visualized on stage (Act III, for example, opens sixteen years after the close of Act II; during this time a white daughter was born to

Virginia: "Há 15 anos nasceu uma filha"–p. 169 [Fifteen years ago a daughter was born]; the setting has changed little as darkness still pervades the house of Ismael: "Há 16 anos que não faz sol nesta casa. Há 16 anos que é noite"–p. 170 [It has been sixteen years since there was sun in this house. For sixteen years it has been night]). More important, however, is the fact that the chorus is symbolic of theater itself; it emphasizes the theatricality of the text, drawing attention to the work as theater rather than reality. The group of black women, always present on the stage, constitutes a symbolic sign of contrast between real and unreal, while serving the usual functions of a chorus. They are unreal in terms of the "real" characters of the fictive world, and their prophetic and litany-like language, which is heard directly or perceived as a background sound (e.g., when the playwright indicates that "Perdem-se as vozes num murmúrio de prece"–p. 170 [The voices are lost in the murmur of prayer], as he does after they have spoken directly) is theatrical in nature as opposed to the more realistic dialogue of the characters.

The sign vehicles create certain interpretants that change as the functions of the signs are perceived differently by the spectator. The spectator is constantly in the process of perceiving the signs and having to revise his understanding of them. At first, for example, he sees the beds as indices of a particular space, and the contrast of the made and unmade beds is uncertain until it is explained in the dialogue. The spectator sees the beds as signs of a bedroom, but the contrast is a sign for which the interpretant is not readily available. When it is available, it is the interpretant of a sign more complex than would be necessary to indicate only a physical location. The unmade bed is the one where Ismael first raped Virginia eight years before the opening of the play. He has not allowed the bed to be changed; it is there as a constant reminder of that first night. The made bed is symbolic of marriage and order, the unmade one of rape, violence, disorder. However, the beds are equated through the dialogue when it is learned that every night is like the original night; Virginia feels raped every night that Ismael makes love to her ("amor com um homem assim é o mesmo que ser violada todos os dias"–p. 143 [love with a man like that is the same as being raped every day]). Both beds then become symbolic of dominance in the traditional sense of male-female, and in the non-traditional sense of black-white. It is in both beds that the black Ismael dominates the white Virginia. However, the beds later become symbolic in another sense, as different interpretants of the same sign vehicles are made possible. As Virginia and Ismael are reduced to the same being, the question of illusion and reality enters: Is it really rape or not? Who is dominating whom? Are the emotions love or hate? Is it indeed possible to separate these at certain levels of being? The beds become a sign of paradox, a sign of the play of oppositions throughout the entire text, and even relate to the opposition of life and death; the bed is where the black children who will inevitably die are conceived. The black dress on Virginia and the white suit Ismael wears are also part of the underlying opposition and paradox; Virginia is not the personification of goodness and innocence, as Ismael is not a sign of total evil and corruption. The contrast of black costume on white skin and white costume on black person thus symbolizes an equation of the two characters in their human and mythical condition. The process that occurs on stage may be characterized as what Pladott calls iconic elements functioning in an essentially symbolic system; these elements, such as the few scenic metonymies used to create a notion of space, are foregrounded and deautomatized. Through this process the elements become symbolic, pointing to something beyond their iconic and indexical functions and creating new dimensions of meaning (cf. Pladott 1982: 38).

Is the world the playwright creates on stage a dark world of sinister, evil forces? Is it the mythic world in which archetypal beings play out their destinies? Or is it an icon of the unconscious mind in which the individual lives out emotions and fantasies that cannot surface in the world of the conscious mind? The stage, in any case, is a sign, and its object is the human mind at a certain level of consciousness, a level of firstness itself, as is the world Ismael attempts to create. Over the course of the text it is obvious that the playwright does not simply present characters and situations of interest; he presents a text in which the element of self-reflexivity is perhaps most important. His theater is one of how theater comes to signify.

Nelson's theater, in general, is characterized by this tendency, and thus is like much of contemporary theater, which "is concerned not only with signifying but also with a reflexive discourse about the very processes by which it signifies" (Avigal and Rimmon-Kennan 1981: 11). It is a theater in which "objects function. . . both at the level of discourse and at that of meta-discourse" (ibid).

The worlds constructed by Nelson's characters parallel the fictional world of the text, turning the entire text into a sign of self-reflection. The text becomes a sign of its own creation, a sign of its own fiction, a mixture of the real and the fictive. The work is a metafiction; it "self-consciously and systematically draws attention to its status as an artefact in order to pose questions about the relationship between fiction and reality" (Waugh 1984: 2). However, unlike much of contemporary theater, Nelson's text achieves this in a subtle manner, without specific references to theater within the play or through actors stepping out of character and commenting on the work. The last world Ismael attempts to create is a prime example of this subtlety: the world of the glass mausoleum for himself and Ana Maria. The prop is visualized on stage thus creating an impact greater than if it were simply referred to in the verbal code. The spectator actually views the object that is to be the final world of these characters and actually sees the final enclosure of Ana Maria. This world is the final comment of the text on theater and life, and it is perhaps the strongest because of the dramatic situation surrounding it. The glass mausoleum evokes the image of Snow White, in which the person within the mausoleum is dead but can be magically revived. The world of the glass mausoleum in Nelson's text parallels the theatrical text in that it is a world which one can observe but in which one cannot directly participate. The person (or persons) within the mausoleum are dead to the world and observers outside it, as the characters of the theatrical text are dead to the nonfictional world. However, in the case of Snow White and the world of the theater, both may be revived under magical conditions: either by a kiss or by a performance.

The physical space confiscated and separated from its real surroundings for the performance becomes a space of paradox. It is a real space peopled by real beings, speaking a real language, wearing real clothes. These real elements, however, are used to create an illusion, a world that does not exist in reality, but only in the space set aside to represent the illusion of real space. States (1985: 202) captures this notion well in speaking of the relationship between actor and audience, using the spectator's recognition upon completion of the performance that Hamlet was a fiction, "a vivid lie":

> Here we are brought against two overlapping paradoxes of the theater: that something so intensely real could lack the funda-

mental quality of the real (endurance); and that something so absolute as the history of Hamlet could be contained in a "local habitation" (technically, a theater stage) as a kind of brief seizure in the real.

The stage, its objects, and the actors are simply signs, vehicles for the unreal, the absent or nonexistent of the fictive world of the text. The real is used to create the unreal. Nelson uses this paradoxical space to exploit not only his sense of innovation and renovation for the Brazilian stage in terms of technical and thematic aspects, but also to work out what seems to be his own sense or need to understand how real people manipulate and create their own realities and how fragile these are when perceived by others who, in turn, have their own worlds and realities. It is on the stage that he can attempt to reconcile irreconcilable dualities that haunt the human being (i.e., life/death, love/hate, real/unreal), and he does this by showing that they are not reconcilable, that indeed they cannot be reconciled because they cannot even be concretely defined in terms of meaning. Meanings shift as signs are perceived differently by different individuals, thus the world outside the theater, and the world(s) within it, are composed of a complex of ever-shifting signs that the spectator/participant must confront and attempt to order and understand at each moment of existence.

REFERENCES

Alter, Jean (1981). "From text to performance." *Poetics Today* 2 (3), 113-139.
—— (1987). "Waiting for the referent. Waiting for Godot? On referring in theatre." In *On Referring in Literature*, Anna Whiteside and Michael Issacharoff (eds.), 42-56. Bloomington: Indiana University Press.
Anspach, Sílvia Simone (1987). *Peter Shaffer e Nelson Rodrigues: A dupla face de um signo*. Unpublished Ph. D. dissertation, Pontifícia Universidade Católica de São Paulo.
Arrowsmith, William (1974). "Chorus." In *Princeton Encyclopedia of Poetry and Poetics*, Alex Preminger et. al. (eds.), 124-5. Princeton: Princeton University Press.
Avigal, Shoshana and Rimmon-Kennan, Shlomith (1981). "What do Brook's bricks mean? Toward a theory of the mobility of objects in theatrical discourse." *Poetics Today* 2 (3), 11-34.
Barrettini, Célia (1980). *O teatro de ontem e hoje*. São Paulo: Editora Perspectiva.
Barthes, Roland (1972). *Critical Essays*, trans. by Richard Howard. Evanston: Northwestern University Press.
—— (1981). *Camera Lucida*, trans. by Richard Howard. New York: Wang and Hill.
Bassnett-McGuire, Susan (1980). "An introduction to theater semiotics." *Theatre Quarterly* 10 (38), 47-53.
Bazin, André (1967). *What Is Cinema?* Vol. I. Berkeley: University of California Press.
Berger, John (1980). *About Looking*. New York: Pantheon Books.
Bogatyrev, Petr (1976a). "Forms and function of folk theater." In *Semiotics of Art: Prague School Contributions*, Ladislav Matejka and Irwin Titunik (eds.), 51-56. Cambridge, Mass.: MIT Press. (First published in 1940)
—— (1976b). "Semiotics in the folk theatre." In *Semiotics of Art: Prague School Contributions*, Ladislav Matejka and Irwin Titunik (eds.), 33-49. Cambridge, Mass.: MIT press. (First published in 1938).
Buczynska-Garewicz, Hanna (1981). "The intepretant and a system of signs." *Ars Semeiotica* 4 (2), 187-200.
—— (1982). "Sign versus the perfect beginning." In *Studies in Peirce's Semiotic*, David Savan (ed.), 5-24. Toronto: Toronto Semiotic Circle. Monographs, Working Papers and Prepublications, No. 3.
—— (1983). "The reality of signs." *Semiotica* 45 (3/4), 315-330.
Calabrese, Omar (1986). "Photography. History." In *Encyclopedic Dictionary of Semiotics*. Thomas A. Sebeok (ed.), 723-24. Berlin: Mouton de Gruyter.
Cardoso Gomes, Valderez (1981). *Nelson Rodrigues e o eterno retorno*. São Paulo: Grupo de Teatro Macunaíma.

Carlson, Marvin (1985). "Theater as event." *Semiotica* 56 (3/4), 309-14.
Chaudhuri, Una (1984). "The spectator in drama/drama in the spectator." *Modern Drama* 27 (3), 281-298.
—— (1986). *No Man's Stage: A Semiotic Study of Jean Genet's Major Plays*. Ann Arbor: UMI Research Press.
Clark, Fred M. and Gazolla de García, Ana Lucía (1978). *Twentieth-Century Brazilian Theater: Essays*. Chapel Hill, N. C.: Estudios de Hispanófila.
Coppieters, Frank (1981). "Performance and perception." *Poetics Today* 2 (3), 35-48.
Culler, Jonathan (1983). *Roland Barthes*. New York: Oxford University Press.
Deely, John (1985). *Logic as a Liberal Art*. Toronto: Toronto Semiotic Circle Monographs, Working Papers, and Prepublications, No. 2.
De Marinis, Marco (1978). "Lo spettacolo come testo (I)." *Versus* 21, 66-104.
—— (1983). "Theatrical comprehension: A socio-semiotic approach." *Theater* 15 (1), 12-17.
—— (1985). "Toward a cognitive semiotic of theatrical emotions." *Versus* 41, 5-19.
—— (1986). "Theater." In *Encyclopedic Dictionary of Semiotics*, Thomas A. Sebeok (ed.), 1088-91. Berlin: Mouton de Gruyter.
—— (1987). "Dramaturgy of the spectator." *The Drama Review* 31 (2), 100-114.
De Toro, Fernando (1987). *Semiótica del teatro*. Buenos Aires: Editorial Galerna.
Dubois, Philippe (1983). *L'Acte Photographique*. Paris and Brussels: Nathan and Labor.
Eco, Umberto (1976). *A Theory of Semiotics*. Bloomington: Indiana University Press.
—— (1977). "Semiotics of theatrical performance." *The Drama Reveiw* 21 (1), 107-17.
—— (1984). *Semiotics and the Philosophy of Language*. Bloomington: Indiana University Press.
Elam, Keir (1977). "Language in the theater." *Sub-Stance* 18/19, 139-62.
—— (1980). *The Semiotics of Theatre and Drama*. London and New York: Methuen.
—— (1988). "Much ado about doing things with words (and other means): Some problems in the pragmatics of theatre and drama." In *Performing Texts*, Michael Issacharoff and Robin F. Jones (eds.), 39-58. Philadelphia: University of Pennsylvania Press.
Esslin, Martin (1982). "The stage: Reality, symbol, metaphor." In *Drama and Symbolism*, James Redmond (ed.), 1-12. Cambridge: Cambridge University Press.
—— (1987). *The Field of Drama*. London: Methuen.
Evans, Donald (1978). "Photographs and primitive signs." *Proceedings of the Aristotelian Society* 79, 213-38.
Feral, Josette (1982). "Performance and theatricality: The subject demystified." *Modern Drama* 25 (1), 170-81.
Figueiredo, Guilherme (1975). "*Vestido de noiva*, de Nelson Rodrigues, no Municipal pelos 'Comediantes'." *Dionysos* 24 (22), 109-112. (Reprinted from *Correio da Manhã*, 1948).
Fisch, Max (1986). *Peirce, Semeiotic and Pragmatism: Essays*, Kenneth Lane Ketner and Christian J. W. Kloesel (eds.). Bloomington: Indiana University Press.
Fischer-Lichte, Erika (1982). "The theatrical code. An approach to the problem." In *Multimedial Communication*, Vol. II: *Theatre Semiotics*, Ernest W. B. Hess-Luttich (ed.), 46-62. Tubingen: Gunter Narr Verlag.
—— (1987). "The performance as an 'interpretant' of the drama." *Semiotica* 64 (3/4), 197-212.
Gorlée, Dinda L. (1987). "Firstness, Secondness, Thirdness, and Cha(u)nciness." *Semiotica* 65 (1/2), 45-55.

Gulli Pugliatti, Paola (1976). *I segni latenti: Scrittura come virtualità in King Lear.* Messina and Florence: D'Anna.

Hall, Edward T. (1966). *The Hidden Dimension.* New York: Doubleday.

Helbo, André (1977). "Theater as representation." *Sub-Stance* 18 (19), 172-81.

——— (1987). *Theory of the Performing Arts.* Philadelphia: John Benjamins.

Holowka, Teresa (1984). "On conventionality of signs and semiotic simplification." In *Sign, System and Function,* Jerzy Pelc et al. (eds.), 69-75. Berlin: Mouton.

Holub, Robert C. (1984). *Reception Theory.* London and New York: Methuen.

Hornby, Richard (1986). *Drama, Metadrama, and Perception.* Lewisburg, Pa.: Bucknell University Press.

Hume, Kathryn (1984). *Fantasy and Mimesis. Responses to Reality in Western Literature.* London and New York: Methuen.

Ingarden, Roman (1973). "The functions of language in the theatre." In *The Literary Work of Art,* trans. by George G. Grabowicz, 377-396. Evanston, Ill.: Northwestern University Press.

Issacharoff, Michael (1981). "Drama and the reader." *Poetics Today* 2 (3), 255-63.

——— (1988a). "Stage codes." In *Performing Texts,* Michael Issacharoff and Robin F. Jones (eds.), 59-74. Philadelphia: University of Pennsylvania Press.

——— (1988b). "Postscript or pinch of salt: Performance as mediation or deconstruction." In *Performing Texts,* Michael Issacharoff and Robin F. Jones (eds.), 138-143. Philadelphia: University of Pennsylvania Press.

Jakobson, Roman (1987a). "Dada." In *Language in Literature,* Krystyna Pomorska and Stephen Rudy (eds.), 34-40. Cambridge: Harvard University Press (First published in 1921).

——— (1987b). "Futurism." In *Language in Literature,* Krystyna Pomorska and Stephen Rudy (eds.), 28-33. Cambridge: Harvard University Press (First published in 1919).

——— (1987c). "On realism." In *Language in Literature,* Krystyna Pomorska and Stephen Rudy (eds.), 19-27. Cambridge: Harvard University Press (First published in 1921).

Johansen, Jorgen Dines (1985). "Prolegomena to a semiotic theory of text interpretation." *Semiotica* 57 (3/4), 225-88.

——— (1986a). "The place of semiotics in the study of literature." In *Semiotics and International Scholarship: Towards a Language of Theory,* Jonathan D. Evans and André Helbo (eds.), 101-126. Dordrecht: Martinus Nijhoff Publishers.

——— (1986b). "Umberto Eco's platform." In *Approches de l'opéra,* André Helbo (ed.), 183-190. Paris: Didier Erudition.

Johansen, Jorgen Dines and Wiingaard, Jytte (1982). "Description and depiction. On the indexical function of the icon in the staging of Ibsen's *The Master Builder.*" *Degrés* 31, f-f8.

Kirby, Michael (1987). *A Formalist Theatre.* Philadelphia: University of Pennsylvania Press.

Kott, Jan (1969). "The icon and the absurd." *The Drama Review* 14, 17-24.

Kowzan, Tadeusz (1968). "The sign in the theatre." *Diogenes* 61, 52-80.

Kuhner, Maria Helena (1971). *Teatro em tempo de síntese.* Rio de Janeiro: Editora Paz e Terra.

Kuznicka, Danuta (1986). "The deep structure of theatrical performance." In *Approches de l'Opéra,* André Helbo (ed.), 139-144. Paris: Didier Erudition.

Larsen, Svend Erik (1985). "The symbol of the knife in Buchner's *Woyzeck.*" *Orbis Litterarum* 40, 258-281.

Lima Lins, Ronaldo (1979). *O teatro de Nelson Rodrigues.* Rio de Janeiro: Livraria Francisco Alves.

Lins, Álvaro (1975). "Algumas notas sobre 'Os Comediantes'." *Dionysos* 24 (22), 61-68 (Transcribed from *Correio da Manhã* 2/1/1944).
Magaldi, Sábato (1962). *Panorama do teatro brasileiro*. São Paulo: Difusão Européia do Livro.
—— (1967). "Teatro: marco zero." In Oswald de Andrade, *O rei da vela*, 7-16. São Paulo: Difusão Europeia do Livro.
—— (1981a). "Introdução." In *Teatro completo de Nelson Rodrigues*, Vol. I, 7-38. Rio de Janeiro: Editora Nova Fronteira.
—— (1981b). "Introdução." In *Teatro completo de Nelson Rodrigues*, Vol. II, 13-48. Rio de Janeiro: Editora Nova Fronteira.
—— (1985). "Prefácio." In *Teatro completo de Nelson Rodrigues*, Vol. III, 7-47. Rio de Janeiro: Editora Nova Fronteira.
—— (1987). *Nelson Rodrigues: Dramaturgia e encenações*. São Paulo: Editora Perspectiva/Editora da Universidade de São Paulo.
Metz, Christian (1985). "Photography and fetish." *October* 34, 81-90.
Mounin, Georges (1986). "Photography. Theory." In *Encyclopedic Dictionary of Semiotics*, Thomas A. Sebeok (ed.), 721-23. Berlin: Mouton de Gruyter.
Nuttall, A. D. (1983). *A New Mimesis. Shakespeare and the Representation of Reality*. London and New York: Methuen.
Orvell, Miles (1980). "Reproduction and 'The Real Thing': The anxiety of realism in the age of photography." In *The Technological Imagination: Theories and Fictions*, Teresa de Lauretis et al. (eds.), 49-64. Madison, Wis.: Coda Press.
Pagnini, Marcello (1987). *The Pragmatics of Literature*, trans. by Nancy Jones-Henry. Bloomington: Indiana University Press.
Pavis, Patrice (1981). "Problems of a semiology of theatrical gesture." *Poetics Today* 2 (3), 65-93.
—— (1982). *Languages of the Stage*. New York: Performing Arts Journal Publications.
—— (1985). "La réception du texte dramatique et spectaculaire: Les processus de fictionnalisation et d'idéologisation." *Versus* 41, 69-94.
—— (1987). "Production, reception, and the social context." In *On Referring in Literature*, Anna Whiteside and Michael Issacharoff (eds.), 122-137. Bloomington: Indiana University Press.
—— (1988). "From text to performance." In *Performing Texts*, Michael Issacharoff and Robin F. Jones (eds.), 86-100. Philadelphia: University of Pennsylvania Press.
Peirce, Charles S. (1931-1958). *The Collected Papers of Charles Sanders Peirce*, Vols. I-VI, Charles Hartshorne, Paul Weiss (eds.); Vols. VII-VIII, Arthur W. Burkes (ed.). Cambridge: Harvard University Press. References to the *Collected Papers* are indicated in parentheses by volume and paragraph number respectively. In quoting from the unpublished manuscripts, I have indicated the manuscript number and pagination made by scholars from the Institute for Studies in Pragmaticism, Texas Tech University, Lubbock, Texas.
—— (1977). *Semiotics and Significs. The Correspondence between Charles S. Peirce and Victoria Lady Welby*, Charles S. Hardwick (ed.). Bloomington: Indiana University Press.
Pelegrino, Hélio (1966). "A obra e *O beijo no asfalto*." In Nelson Rodrigues, *Teatro quase completo*, Vol. IV, 9-25. Rio de Janeiro: Edições Tempo Brasileiro.
Pinto, Júlio (1989). *The Reading of Time. A Semantico-Semiotic Approach*. Berlin: Mouton de Gruyter.
Pladott, Dinnah (1982). "The dynamics of the sign systems in the theatre." In *Multimedial Communication*, Vol. II: *Theatre Semiotics*, Ernest W. B. Hess-Luttich (ed.), 28-45. Tubingen: Gunter Narr Verlag.

Pontes, Joel (1966). "Dramaturgia contemporânea no Brasil." *Luso-Brazilian Review* 3 (2), 25-42.
Prado, Décio de Almeida (1968). "Evolução da literatura dramática." In *A literatura no Brasil*, Vol. 6, Afrânio Coutinha (ed.), 7-37. Rio de Janeiro: Editorial Sul Americana.
——— (1975). "O teatro." In *O modernismo*, Affonso Ávila (ed.), 139-150. São Paulo: Editora Perspectiva.
——— (1988). *O teatro brasileiro moderno*. São Paulo: Editora Perspectiva e Editora da Universidade de São Paulo.
Quigley, Austin E. (1985). *The Modern Stage and Other Worlds*. New York: Methuen.
Ransdell, Joseph (1976). "Another interpretation of Peirce's semiotic." *Transactions of the Charles S. Peirce Society* 12 (2), 97-110.
——— (1977). "Some leading ideas of Peirce's semiotic." *Semiotica* 19 (3/4), 157-178.
——— (1986). "Charles Sanders Peirce." In *Encyclopedic Dictionary of Semiotics*, Thomas A. Sebeok (ed.), 637-695. Berlin: Mouton de Gruyter.
Ribeiro, Leo Gilson (1966). "O sol sobre o pântano. Nelson Rodrigues, um expressionista brasileiro." In Nelson Rodrigues, *Teatro quase completo*, 377-92. Rio de Janeiro: Edições Tempo Brasileiro.
Rodrigues, Nelson (1949). "Teatro desagradável." *Dionysos* I, 16-21.
——— (1977a). *O reacionário*. Rio de Janeiro: Editora Record.
——— (1977b). *Vestido de noiva*. São Paulo: Abril Cultura.
——— (1980). *The Wedding Dress*, trans. by Fred M. Clark. Valencia: Ediciones-Albatros Hispanófila (Translation of *Vestido de noiva*).
——— (1981a). *Teatro completo de Nelson Rodrigues*, Vol. I. Rio de Janeiro: Editora Nova Fronteira.
——— (1981b). *Teatro completo de Nelson Rodrigues*, Vol. II. Rio de Janeiro: Editora Nova Fronteira.
——— (1985). *Teatro completo de Nelson Rodrigues*, Vol. III. Rio de Janeiro: Editora Nova Fronteira.
——— (1989). *Teatro completo de Nelson Rodrigues*. Vol. IV. Rio de Janeiro: Editora Nova Fronteira.
Rokem, Freddie (1986). *Theatrical Space in Ibsen, Chekhov and Strindberg*. Ann Arbor: UMI Research Press.
Rozik, Eli (1983). "Theatre as language: A semiotic approach." *Semiotica* 45 (1/2), 65-87.
Ruffini, Franco (1978). *Semiotica del testo: L'esempio teatro*. Rome: Bulzoni.
Schogt, Henry G. (1988) *Linguistics, Literary Analysis, and Literary Translation*. Toronto: University of Toronto Press.
Scott, F. (1983). "Process from the Peircean point of view: Some applications to art." *American Journal of Semiotics* 2 (1/2), 157-74.
Thomas A. Sebeok (1979). *The Sign & Its Masters*. Austin: University of Texas Press.
Serpieri, Alessandro (1978). "Ipotesi teorica di segmentazione del testo teatrale." In *Come comunica il teatro: Dal testo alla scena*. Alessandro Serpieri et al. (eds.), 11-54. Milan: Il Formichiere.
Serpieri, Alessandro et al. (1981). "Toward a segmentation of the dramatic text." *Poetics Today* 2 (3), 163-200.
Short, T. L. (1981). "Semeiosis and intentionality." *Transactions of the Charles S. Peirce Society* 17 (3), 197-223.
——— (1982). "Life among the legisigns." *Transactions of the Charles S. Peirce Society* 18 (4), 285-310.

Simonson, Lee (1979). "The ideas of Adolph Appia." In *The Theory of the Modern Stage*, Eric Bentley (ed.), 27-50. New York: Penguin Books.
States, Bert O. (1985). *Great Reckonings in Little Rooms*. Berkeley: University of California Press.
Sussekind, Maria Flora (1977). "Nelson Rodrigues e o fundo falso." In *I Concurso Nacional de Monografias-1976*, 7-42. Brasília: Ministério da Educação e Cultura.
Tomas, David (1982). "The ritual of photography." *Semiotica* 40 (1/2), 1-25.
—— (1983). "A mechanism for meaning: A ritual and the photographic process." *Semiotica* 46 (1), 1-39.
Ubersfeld, Anne (1977). *Lire le théâtre*. Paris: Editions Sociales.
Van Zyl, John (1979). "Towards a socio-semiotic of performance." *Semiotic Scene* 3 (2), 99-111.
Veltruský, Jiří (1964). "Man and object in the theater." In *A Prague School Reader on Esthetics, Literary Structure and Style*, Paul L. Garvin (ed.), 83-91. Washington: Georgetown University Press (First published in 1940).
Waugh, Patricia (1984). *Metafiction. The Theory and Practice of Self-Conscious Fiction*. London and New York: Methuen.
Whiteside, Anna (1988). "Self-referring artifacts." In *Performing Texts*. Michael Issacharoff and Robin F. Jones (eds.), 27-38. Philadelphia: University of Pennsylvannia Press.
Zeman, Jay (1977a). "The esthetic sign in Peirce's semiotic theory." *Semiotica* 19 (3/4), 241-258.
—— (1977b). "Peirce's theory of signs." In *A Perfusion of Signs*. Thomas A. Sebeok (ed.), 22-39. Bloomington: Indiana University Press.
Ziembinski, Zbigniew (1975). "Os comediantes—marco novo." *Dionysos* 24 (22), 54-56.

NORTH CAROLINA STUDIES IN THE ROMANCE LANGUAGES AND LITERATURES

I.S.B.N. Prefix 0-8078-

Recent Titles

RICHARD SANS PEUR, EDITED FROM "LE ROMANT DE RICHART" AND FROM GILLES CORROZET'S "RICHART SANS PAOUR", by Denis Joseph Conlon. 1977. (No. 192). *-9192-4.*

MARCEL PROUST'S GRASSET PROOFS. *Commentary and Variants,* by Douglas Alden. 1978. (No. 193). *-9193-2.*

MONTAIGNE AND FEMINISM, by Cecile Insdorf. 1977. (No. 194). *-9194-0.*

SANTIAGO F. PUGLIA, AN EARLY PHILADELPHIA PROPAGANDIST FOR SPANISH AMERICAN INDEPENDENCE, by Merle S. Simmons. 1977. (No. 195). *-9195-9.*

BAROQUE FICTION-MAKING. A STUDY OF GOMBERVILLE'S "POLEXANDRE", by Edward Baron Turk. 1978. (No. 196). *-9196-7.*

THE TRAGIC FALL: DON ÁLVARO DE LUNA AND OTHER FAVORITES IN SPANISH GOLDEN AGE DRAMA, by Raymond R. MacCurdy. 1978. (No. 197). *-9197-5.*

A BAHIAN HERITAGE. An Ethnolinguistic Study of African Influences on Bahian Portuguese, by William W. Megenney. 1978. (No. 198). *-9198-3.*

"LA QUERELLE DE LA ROSE": Letters and Documents, by Joseph L. Baird and John R. Kane. 1978. (No. 199). *-9199-1.*

TWO AGAINST TIME. *A Study of the Very Present Worlds of Paul Claudel and Charles Péguy,* by Joy Nachod Humes. 1978. (No. 200). *-9200-9.*

TECHNIQUES OF IRONY IN ANATOLE FRANCE. Essay on *Les Sept Femmes de la Barbe-Bleue,* by Diane Wolfe Levy. 1978. (No. 201). *-9201-7.*

THE PERIPHRASTIC FUTURES FORMED BY THE ROMANCE REFLEXES OF "VADO (AD)" PLUS INFINITIVE, by James Joseph Champion. 1978. (No. 202). *-9202-5.*

THE EVOLUTION OF THE LATIN /b/-/u̯/ MERGER: A Quantitative and Comparative Analysis of the *B-V* Alternation in Latin Inscriptions, by Joseph Louis Barbarino. 1978. (No. 203). *-9203-3.*

METAPHORIC NARRATION: THE STRUCTURE AND FUNCTION OF METAPHORS IN "A LA RECHERCHE DU TEMPS PERDU", by Inge Karalus Crosman. 1978. (No. 204). *-9204-1.*

LE VAIN SIECLE GUERPIR. A Literary Approach to Sainthood through Old French Hagiography of the Twelfth Century, by Phyllis Johnson and Brigitte Cazelles. 1979. (No. 205). *-9205-X.*

THE POETRY OF CHANGE: A STUDY OF THE SURREALIST WORKS OF BENJAMIN PÉRET, by Julia Field Costich. 1979. (No. 206). *-9206-8.*

NARRATIVE PERSPECTIVE IN THE POST-CIVIL WAR NOVELS OF FRANCISCO AYALA "MUERTES DE PERRO" AND "EL FONDO DEL VASO", by Maryellen Bieder. 1979. (No. 207). *-9207-6.*

RABELAIS: HOMO LOGOS, by Alice Fiola Berry. 1979. (No. 208). *-9208-4.*

"DUEÑAS" AND "DONCELLAS": A STUDY OF THE "DOÑA RODRÍGUEZ" EPISODE IN "DON QUIJOTE", by Conchita Herdman Marianella. 1979. (No. 209). *-9209-2.*

PIERRE BOAISTUAU'S "HISTOIRES TRAGIQUES": A STUDY OF NARRATIVE FORM AND TRAGIC VISION, by Richard A. Carr. 1979. (No. 210). *-9210-6.*

REALITY AND EXPRESSION IN THE POETRY OF CARLOS PELLICER, by George Melnykovich. 1979. (No. 211). *-9211-4.*

MEDIEVAL MAN, HIS UNDERSTANDING OF HIMSELF, HIS SOCIETY, AND THE WORLD, by Urban T. Holmes, Jr. 1980. (No. 212). *-9212-2.*

MÉMOIRES SUR LA LIBRAIRIE ET SUR LA LIBERTÉ DE LA PRESSE, introduction and notes by Graham E. Rodmell. 1979. (No. 213). *-9213-0.*

THE FICTIONS OF THE SELF. THE EARLY WORKS OF MAURICE BARRES, by Gordon Shenton. 1979. (No. 214). *-9214-9.*

When ordering please cite the *ISBN Prefix* plus the last four digits for each title.

Send orders to: University of North Carolina Press
P.O. Box 2288
CB# 6215
Chapel Hill, NC 27515-2288
U.S.A.

NORTH CAROLINA STUDIES IN THE ROMANCE LANGUAGES AND LITERATURES

I.S.B.N. Prefix 0-8078-

Recent Titles

CECCO ANGIOLIERI. A STUDY, by Gifford P. Orwen. 1979. (No. 215). *-9215-7.*
THE INSTRUCTIONS OF SAINT LOUIS: A CRITICAL TEXT, by David O'Connell. 1979. (No. 216). *-9216-5.*
ARTFUL ELOQUENCE, JEAN LEMAIRE DE BELGES AND THE RHETORICAL TRADITION, by Michael F. O. Jenkins. 1980. (No. 217). *-9217-3.*
A CONCORDANCE TO MARIVAUX'S COMEDIES IN PROSE, edited by Donald C. Spinelli. 1979. (No. 218). 4 volumes, *-9218-1* (set); *-9219-X* (v. 1); *-9220-3* (v. 2); *-9221-1* (v. 3); *-9222-X* (v. 4).
ABYSMAL GAMES IN THE NOVELS OF SAMUEL BECKETT, by Angela B. Moorjani. 1982. (No. 219). *-9223-8.*
GERMAIN NOUVEAU DIT HUMILIS: ÉTUDE BIOGRAPHIQUE, par Alexandre L. Amprimoz. 1983. (No. 220). *-9224-6.*
THE "VIE DE SAINT ALEXIS" IN THE TWELFTH AND THIRTEENTH CENTURIES: AN EDITION AND COMMENTARY, by Alison Goddard Elliot. 1983. (No. 221). *-9225-4.*
THE BROKEN ANGEL: MYTH AND METHOD IN VALÉRY, by Ursula Franklin. 1984. (No. 222). *-9226-2.*
READING VOLTAIRE'S "CONTES": A SEMIOTICS OF PHILOSOPHICAL NARRATION, by Carol Sherman. 1985. (No. 223). *-9227-0.*
THE STATUS OF THE READING SUBJECT IN THE "LIBRO DE BUEN AMOR", by Marina Scordilis Brownlee. 1985. (No. 224). *-9228-9.*
MARTORELL'S "TIRANT LO BLANCH": A PROGRAM FOR MILITARY AND SOCIAL REFORM IN FIFTEENTH-CENTURY CHRISTENDOM, by Edward T. Aylward. 1985. (No. 225). *-9229-7.*
NOVEL LIVES: THE FICTIONAL AUTOBIOGRAPHIES OF GUILLERMO CABRERA INFANTE AND MARIO VARGAS LLOSA, by Rosemary Geisdorfer Feal. 1986. (No. 226). *-9230-0.*
SOCIAL REALISM IN THE ARGENTINE NARRATIVE, by David William Foster. 1986. (No. 227). *-9231-9.*
HALF-TOLD TALES: DILEMMAS OF MEANING IN THREE FRENCH NOVELS, by Philip Stewart. 1987. (No. 228). *-9232-7.*
POLITIQUES DE L'ECRITURE BATAILLE/DERRIDA: le sens du sacré dans la pensée française du surréalisme à nos jours, par Jean-Michel Heimonet. 1987. (No. 229). *-9233-5.*
GOD, THE QUEST, THE HERO: THEMATIC STRUCTURES IN BECKETT'S FICTION, by Laura Barge. 1988. (No. 230). *-9235-1.*
THE NAME GAME. WRITING/FADING WRITER IN "DE DONDE SON LOS CANTANTES", by Oscar Montero. 1988. (No. 231). *-9236-X.*
GIL VICENTE AND THE DEVELOPMENT OF THE COMEDIA, by René Pedro Garay. 1988. (No. 232). *-9234-3.*
HACIA UNA POÉTICA DEL RELATO DIDÁCTICO: OCHO ESTUDIOS SOBRE "EL CONDE LUCANOR", por Aníbal A. Biglieri. 1989. (No. 233). *-9237-8.*
A POETICS OF ART CRITICISM: THE CASE OF BAUDELAIRE, by Timothy Raser. 1989. (No. 234). *-9238-6.*
UMA CONCORDÂNCIA DO ROMANCE "GRANDE SERTÃO: VEREDAS" DE JOÃO GUIMARÃES ROSA, by Myriam Ramsey and Paul Dixon. 1989. (No. 235). Microfiche, *-9239-4.*
CYCLOPEAN SONG: MELANCHOLY AND AESTHETICISM IN GÓNGORA'S "FÁBULA DE POLIFEMO Y GALATEA", by Kathleen Hunt Dolan. 1990. (No. 236). *-9240-8.*
THE "SYNTHESIS" NOVEL IN LATIN AMERICA. A STUDY ON JOÃO GUIMARÃES ROSA'S "GRANDE SERTÃO: VEREDAS", by Eduardo de Faria Coutinho. 1991. (No. 237). *-9241-6.*

When ordering please cite the *ISBN Prefix* plus the last four digits for each title.

Send orders to: University of North Carolina Press
P.O. Box 2288
CB# 6215
Chapel Hill, NC 27515-2288
U.S.A.

The Department of Romance Studies Digital Arts and Collaboration Lab at the University of North Carolina at Chapel Hill is proud to support the digitization of the North Carolina Studies in the Romance Languages and Literatures series.

www.ingramcontent.com/pod-product-compliance
Lightning Source LLC
Chambersburg PA
CBHW030237240426
43663CB00037B/1238